P9-CEV-665

THE
QUALITY
SCHOOL

BOOKS BY WILLIAM GLASSER

Choice Theory: A New Psychology of Personal Freedom

Staying Together

The Quality School Teacher

The Quality School

Choice Theory in the Classroom
(formerly *Control Theory in the Classroom)*

Schools Without Failure

Reality Therapy

Positive Addiction

THE
QUALITY
SCHOOL

Managing Students
Without Coercion

REVISED EDITION

William Glasser, M.D.

HarperPerennial
A Division of HarperCollinsPublishers

THE QUALITY SCHOOL. Copyright © 1990, 1992, 1998 by William Glasser, Inc., Joseph Paul Glasser, Alice Joan Glasser, and Martin Howard Glasser. All rights reserved. Printed in the United States of America. No part of this book may be used or reproduced in any manner whatsoever without written permission except in the case of brief quotations embodied in critical articles and reviews. For information address HarperCollins Publishers, Inc., 10 East 53rd Street, New York, NY 10022.

HarperCollins books may be purchased for educational, business, or sales promotional use. For information please write: Special Markets Department, HarperCollins Publishers, Inc., 10 East 53rd Street, New York, NY 10022.

REVISED EDITION

Designed by Kris Tobiassen

Library of Congress Cataloging-in-Publication Data

Glasser, William, 1925–
    The quality school : managing students without coercion / William Glasser. — rev. ed.
        p. cm.
    Includes bibliographical references.
    ISBN 0-06-095286-5
    1. School management and organization—United States. 2. Quality control—United States. 3. Motivation in education—United States. 4. School improvement programs—United States. I. Title.
    LB2805.G534 1997
    371.2' 00973—dc21   98-12112

98 99 00 01 02 ❖/RRD 10 9 8 7 6 5 4 3 2 1

Contents

Author's Note

Since the publication of this book in 1992, I have changed the name of the theory that governs all I do from Control Theory to Choice Theory[SM*]. I did this because the term control theory is both misleading and hard for people to accept. It was not my term to begin with, and I think changing to the new term, choice theory, will be much more acceptable for both teachers and students. While the name has been changed, everything written about the theory in this book is completely accurate.

Choice theory, however, has been expanded and clarified in my 1998 book, *Choice Theory: A New Psychology of Personal Freedom*. All school personnel should find Chapter 10 of that book, "Schooling, Education and the Quality School," especially helpful. In it, I introduce a great many new ideas that can be very effective in the classroom and will help you to reach students who seem uninterested or even antagonistic to school. If you have any questions about what is written in any of my books or how to get more involved as an individual or as a school with my quality school ideas, write, call, fax, or e-mail me at:

The William Glasser Institute
22024 Lassen Street, Suite 118
Chatsworth, CA 91311

---

*Choice Theory[SM], educational services on human behavior and an examination thereof.

phone: (818) 700-8000
fax: (818) 700-0555
web site: http://www.wglasserinst.com
email: wglasser@wglasserinst.com

Preface

Shayle Uroff,[1] who helped Brad Greene to describe work being done at the Apollo School, gave me the following:

A boss drives. A leader leads.
A boss relies on authority. A leader relies on cooperation.
A boss says "I." A leader says "We."
A boss creates fear. A leader creates confidence.
A boss knows how. A leader shows how.
A boss creates resentment. A leader breeds enthusiasm.
A boss fixes blame. A leader fixes mistakes.
A boss makes work drudgery. A leader makes work interesting.

As you read this book, return to this page periodically and reread these statements. They will help keep you on track.

THE
QUALITY
SCHOOL

CHAPTER ONE

Quality Education Is the Only Answer to Our School Problems

Picture the students in a required academic class at a randomly selected secondary school as a gang of street repair workers. If they were working as hard as the students do in class, half or more would be leaning on their shovels, smoking and socializing, perfectly content to let the others do the work. Of those who were working, few would be working hard, and it is likely that none would be doing high-quality work.

It is apparent, however, that students have thought about quality and have a good idea of what, in their school, is considered quality. I have talked at length to groups of high school students about this subject, and most of them see quality in athletics, music, and drama, a few see it in advanced placement academics or shop classes, but almost none see it in regular classes. While they believe they are capable of doing quality work in class, all but a very few admit that they have never done it and have no plans to do it in the future. The purpose of this book is to explain how to manage students so that a substantial majority do high-quality schoolwork: Nothing less will solve the problems of our schools.

If we accept that the purpose of any organization, public or private, is to build a quality product or perform a quality service, then we must also accept that the workers in the organization must do quality work and that the job of the manager is to see that this occurs. In school, the students are the workers, and right now almost none are doing quality work in class. Those who manage in the schools—teachers who manage students directly and administrators who manage teachers and some students—are in most instances highly dedicated, humane people who have tried very hard but have yet to figure out how to manage so that students do significant amounts of quality work.

Is this problem unsolvable? Should we, as we seem to be doing, give up on the idea of many students doing quality work and instead increase the amount of low-quality work—as we do when we settle for trying to reduce the number of dropouts? But if quality education is what we need, does it make that much difference whether a student stays in school and "leans on his shovel" or drops out and "leans on his shovel"?

Or should we look for organizations in which almost all the workers are working hard and doing a quality job and try to apply to the schools what the managers in these places are doing? Although not widely known or applied in this country, there are far better management practices than most school managers know about. This book describes these highly successful practices and explains how school managers can learn to use them. What is significant about these practices is that they are specifically aimed at persuading workers to do quality work. In today's competitive world, only organizations whose products and services are high quality thrive, and our schools are far from thriving.

Among those who have taught managers to manage so that almost all workers do high-quality work, one name stands out. To quote from Dr. Myron Tribus, one of his disciples:

> The man who taught the Japanese to achieve high quality at low cost (after World War II) is an American, Dr. W. Edwards Deming. . . . The Japanese faced an "export or die" situation. They had a reputation for shoddy products. . . . With the aid of the MacArthur government, they located Dr. Deming, and he proceeded to teach them the methods rejected by our managers. The rest is history.[1]

What this history tells us is that the Japanese workers, led by managers trained by Dr. Deming, for the first time in modern history made very high-quality products, especially automobiles and electronics, available at a price the average person could afford. Given the opportunity to get high quality for the same price as low quality, consumers are stampeding toward "made in Japan," and the result is that Japan is now one of the world's richest countries.

I must mention that today, many years after Dr. Deming introduced his ideas so successfully in Japan, some people have become critical of both how the Japanese now manage and of American managers who claim to be using the same ideas.[2] When this criticism is examined, however, it becomes clear that what is being criticized is not what Dr. Deming taught but rather the distortion of his noncoercive ideas by managers who are only paying lip service to

Deming as they return to the traditional, coercive management practices that have been associated with the problems Deming has shown how to solve.

This book will explain how Dr. Deming's ideas can be brought undistorted into our schools so that the present elitist system, in which just a few students are involved in high-quality work, will be replaced by a system in which almost all students have this experience. Once they do have this experience, which for almost all of them would be a totally new one, students will find it highly satisfying. They will no more turn down the chance to continue doing this kind of work than does the well-managed factory worker. But further, as I will soon explain, students are not only the workers in the school, they are also the products. Once they see that they themselves are gaining in quality, they will make an effort to continue this option, just as we continue to buy the quality products of Japan.

Deming, before his death in 1994, labored for thirty years in Japan before more than a few American industrialists paid attention to him. More are now listening because they have become aware that paying attention to what he had to say may mean their very survival, but teachers and administrators have no such incentive. They have every reason to believe that they will survive whether or not they change what they have done for so long. So as much as Deming's ideas are likely to increase the quality of our education, moving "managing for quality" into practice in our schools will not be easy.

To help administrators and teachers to accept these new management ideas, I will explain the principles of choice theory, with which I have been identified for well over ten years. Choice theory reveals, far better than any existing theory, both why and how all of us behave. It explains both why Deming's ideas, when they are used correctly, work so well and how these ideas can be brought into schools. I do not believe those who manage students will make any major changes in what they do if they do not clearly understand the reasons for these changes. Therefore, choice theory, as it relates to managing for quality, will be explained in detail beginning in Chapter Four.

To me there is a remarkable parallel between the American manufacturers who ignored Deming's suggestion that they make quality their number-one priority after World War II and our seeming lack of concern today that only a few students in any secondary school do what we, or even they, would call high-quality schoolwork. Like the automakers in the seventies who concentrated on building low-quality, high-profit cars and might have gone bankrupt had competition been unrestricted, our schools have focused on trying to get more students to do enough work, even though that work is almost never high quality, to reach the low-quality standard required for graduation. But, for reasons I will explain in this book, as long as our goal is to "get more of them to do enough to get through," we will only fall further behind.

This claim is confirmed by the disturbing reports printed almost daily in our newspapers that show American college students to be in the minority among graduate students in math and science in our own country; foreign students predominate. And as flawed as any machine-scored tests may be, the latest studies show that American thirteen-year-olds, whose scores on achievement tests have been dropping steadily, now rank below almost all their counterparts in the rest of the world in math and science.[3]

As difficult as this is for most teachers to believe, I contend that this continuing drop is caused by the fact that our traditional system of managing students sends a clear message to almost all students that low-quality work is acceptable. Probably fewer than 15 percent of those who attend do quality academic work in school, and even many of these do far less than they are capable of doing. We fail to realize that the way we manage ignores the fact that very few people—and students are no exception—will expend the effort needed to do high-quality work unless they believe that there is quality in what they are asked to do.

While the manager cannot make people do quality work—choice theory contends that no one can make anyone do anything—it is the job of the manager to manage so that the workers or the students can easily see a strong connection between what they are asked to do and what they believe is quality. And as long as we continue to embrace expediency ("get them through") as an excuse to compromise on quality, our schools, already behind, will continue to slip.

That we are not doing this is supported by the fact that many public school teachers, desperate for better education for their own children, are strapping themselves financially to send their children to private schools, which they believe are doing a better job of quality education than the public schools. This is not to say that private schools are actually better than public schools, but only that they are perceived to be so by many people, including many teachers.

It would be extremely difficult to come up with an exact definition of quality education that would apply to all situations. Even without being able to define it, however, we can almost always recognize quality when we see it. Ask any school administrator to take you through the school and show you some high-quality work in any subject area, and I am certain that you will agree that what you are shown is quality. What is similar about all this work is that none of it could be graded or evaluated by machines—quality never can. Further, as I will explain later when I discuss choice theory, it is almost impossible for us to do or see anything without making a fairly accurate appraisal of the quality of what we see or do.

Throughout the rest of this book, I will continue to use the industrial analogy of workers and managers because I think it is both accurate and appropriate. The students are the workers of the school, and high-quality work, whether it is waiting on tables or academics, is the difference between the success or failure of the organization. The teachers are the first-level managers, and the administrators are middle- and upper-level managers. As in industry, the productivity of any school depends mostly on the skill of those who directly manage the workers—the teachers. But according to Deming, their success depends almost completely on how well they, in turn, are managed by the administrators above them.

In his 1982 book, addressed to industry but whose message applies even more urgently to the schools, Deming says, "This book teaches the transformation that is required for survival, a transformation that can only be accomplished by man. A company cannot buy its way into quality—it must be led into quality by top management. A theory of management now exists. Never again may anyone say that there is nothing new in management to teach."[4]

Most of those concerned with the problems of our schools have not focused as specifically on how students are managed as I will in this book. When pressed for a solution, both professionals and nonprofessionals say better teaching is the answer, without realizing that much of what they consider better teaching is really better managing. They call for better teaching because we all remember, regardless of the course, working harder and learning more from some teachers than from others. We also remember thinking how good it would have been to have had more teachers like those.

Our main complaint as students (and this has not changed) was not that the work was too hard, but that it was boring, and this complaint was and still is valid. "Boring" usually meant that we could not relate what we were asked to do with how we might use it in our lives. For example, it is deadly boring to memorize facts that neither we, nor anyone we know, will ever use except for a test in school. The most obvious measure of the effective teachers we remember is that they were not boring; somehow or other what they asked us to do was satisfying to us.

Here perhaps is a major difference between a teacher who understands his or her role as a manager and one who does not; the manager is willing to expend effort to assign work that is not boring because he or she knows that it is almost impossible for bored workers to do high-quality work. As I will explain in Chapter Four when I introduce you to choice theory, the teacher who is a good manager is not boring because he or she has figured out how to teach in a way that makes it easy for students to satisfy their basic needs when they do the work. If teachers do not teach in need-satisfying ways, then they almost all resort to coercion to try to make students learn.

As this book will attempt to explain, effective teachers manage students without coercion. While less effective teachers may be just as concerned about students personally, when they teach they slip into the coercive practices that destroy their effectiveness. Coercive teachers are the rule, not the exception, in our schools. But, if increasing the number of teachers who manage students without coercion, like the good teachers we remember, is the solution to this pressing problem, no one in power seems to want to address this issue.

For example, none of the recommendations in *A Nation at Risk* focused on how teachers managed students. That report claimed that what we needed was a longer school day and year, stiffer graduation requirements, and more homework, all coercive practices.[5] Since it failed to address the fact that longer hours and harder courses with the same teachers for whom students were not now doing quality work would change nothing, it is hardly surprising that this report has not led to any significant improvement in the schools.

What has surfaced that seems effective is a new focus on changing the school structure, and the most popular new configuration is the magnet school. Here, both teachers and students have more choice: Teachers can teach more of what they enjoy, and students can learn more of what interests them. When this occurs, there is no need for coercion. There is already clear evidence that both students and teachers work harder and do more quality work in magnet schools than they do in the less flexible, more coercive neighborhood schools in most school systems.

But, published research documents that magnet schools and other structurally innovative schools can also fail if traditional coercive management prevails. For this reason, many of these schools are now doing much less than they are capable of doing. This is not because their structure is faulty but because, after a good start, many teachers who made a successful effort to improve the way they managed students are being hampered by administrators who tell them that the quality work both they and their students are doing is not acceptable.

And it is not acceptable to administrators, according to the research of Linda McNeil, Professor of Education at Rice University, because it does not include enough of the low-quality schoolwork that state-mandated achievement tests measure.[6] Nothing of high quality, including schoolwork, can be measured by such standard, machine-scored tests. If we were interested in measuring what these successful magnet school teachers are doing, this could easily be done through in-depth interviews, observation of a statistically significant sample by qualified observers, and follow-up studies to see if future academic performance was enhanced by this good work. It is symptomatic of our present self-destructive system that students are made aware in a wide variety of coercive ways that low-quality work that can be measured by machines is the top administrative priority of almost all school systems.

This is beautifully illustrated by the following academic equivalent of the Boston Tea Party:

> A group of seniors at Torrance's academically rigorous West High School intentionally flunked the latest California Assessment Program test in an attempt to send a message to administrators who they believe place too much emphasis on the exam. . . . At the school Wednesday, student body President Kelle Price, who said that she did not intentionally fail the test, said some seniors became disgruntled when some teachers interrupted classes to prepare them for the [state] tests. She said students also believed that administrators—who visited classes to stress the importance of doing well— were too concerned with maintaining the school's image. . . . At West High, there was much debate Wednesday about who—if anyone—places too much emphasis on the tests. Bawden [the principal] blamed the state Department of Education and the press which does not publish other indicators of a school's performance. . . . Bill Franchini, who heads the Torrance Teachers Association, . . . blamed it on a trickle-down effect, saying the pressure starts with the state department . . . and works its way down through the local school districts, principals, teachers and eventually students. "I think they [students] are feeling like pawns in a game that is much bigger than they are," he said.[7]

These assessments are all correct. Intelligent students who want high-quality education are rebelling against the coercion from the top down to do well on low-quality tests. Coercion begets coercion. Anyone who knows history knows this is true.

It is important to be aware that one of the reasons for the success of magnet schools is that there are not too many of them. If there were an attempt to increase their numbers without increasing the number of teachers drawn to them by the opportunity to be free and innovative, there might not be enough teachers to supply many more of these magnet schools. We should keep in mind that the power of innovation is not that it increases the number of effective people, but that it gives the effective people we have a better chance to demonstrate their effectiveness. What magnet schools do that works is far more than structural. When they work, it is because they are also better managed. When they fail, it is usually because they are managed in the traditional coercive way that has produced the low-quality work that predominates now.

Therefore, the shortage of effective teachers is not a problem that can be solved by a new structure. It is caused by how we train and manage teachers and can only be solved by improving the way we do this, no matter what the structure of the school. Teachers who are effective managers will be effective in any school setting, but they will be less effective if they are managed differently from the way they manage students. The good teachers we remember should be especially revered because in most cases they had the strength to manage students far better than they themselves were managed.

If through better administration we can increase the number of effective teachers, we will soon see a wide variety of structural improvements in many schools, improvements made possible and brought about by the increased numbers of more confident, more professional teachers and, because of them, more hard-working students doing quality work. Creating large numbers of magnet schools before improving school management to the point where many more students are involved in quality work is putting the cart before the horse.

This book is about managing schools for quality and, in doing so, moving any school toward being what I will call a quality school. I will focus on how teachers can manage students more effectively and on how administrators can use the same methods to manage teachers. The management method I will suggest is very different from the school management now in place in most schools. As I have already begun to explain, it is based on choice theory and utilizes the proven quality methods of W. Edwards Deming. It is almost unused in schools, although it is being used with great success in a few corporations. The Ford Motor Company may be a particularly apt example.

However, I doubt if the corporations who have improved their management and who are now struggling to maintain what they have accomplished have any idea that what they are doing is explained by a coherent, easily understood theory. As good as Deming's ideas are, it is my belief that they will not spread as widely as needed, or even continue to be used as much as they are, unless many more managers, especially those who manage our schools, realize that they are based on an understandable and usable new theory that is far different from the one most managers use now.

Although there may be the beginnings of a management revolution in a few major industries, these changes are far from widespread, and almost none have reached the schools. Here, as in most industries, teachers and students are being managed in the same way they always have been, the same way that people have been managed for centuries, by a method based on an ancient, "common-sense" theory of how we function, which is best called external control.

But, as I will show when I begin to explain choice theory in Chapter Four, external control theory is wrong. When it is used to manage people, it leads to a traditional management method that I will call boss-management. Boss-management is ineffective because it relies on coercion and always results in the workers and the managers becoming adversaries. Bossing rarely leads to consistent hard work and almost never to quality work, and nowhere is this more obvious than in the schools. Managing for quality demands a new noncoercive method of management that I call lead-management. I will begin to explain this method in detail in Chapter Three.

As many of you know, this is not the first time I have written about the use of choice theory in the schools. *Choice Theory in the Classroom* focused on how the knowledge of this new theory can persuade teachers to use cooperative learning to replace lecturing and individual desk work.[8] But while the feedback on this important change has been very positive, progress has been slow. And it is now apparent to me that progress will continue to be slow until we are able to change from boss-management to lead-management.

Cooperative learning works well because through it students gain power. Lead-managers support this approach because they have discovered that the more they are able to empower workers, the harder they work. In contrast, bosses want to be in charge. They are not comfortable giving workers as much power as cooperative learning requires.

Moving to lead-management, however, means breaking

with tradition, and this is always hard to do. In the schools it will be especially hard, even harder than in industry. As Chapter Two explains, this is because embedded in education is a major obstacle not found in most places where people work.

CHAPTER TWO

Effective Teaching May Be the Hardest Job There Is

I t is unlikely that we will ever move from boss-management to lead-management unless we overcome the obstacle that stands in the way of making this necessary change. This is our failure to understand how difficult it is to teach effectively. We continue to think that if we just buckled down and really tried, we could easily boss our teachers into doing better. Nothing could be further from the truth. What makes this obstacle so difficult to overcome is that most people, educators included, do not see it as an obstacle. Unless it is clearly seen for what it is, there is little chance that we will overcome it and it will continue to block what we must do, which is to change the way we manage both students and teachers.

Almost everyone in our society shares a huge misconception about teaching. By "everyone" I mean not only the general public, but also teachers as well as parents, administrators, school board members, politicians, educational news reporters, and even the college professors who run teacher-preparation programs. What almost all fail to understand is that being an effective teacher may be the most difficult job of all in our society.

Before I explain why this is so, let me define what I believe effective teaching is. An effective teacher is one who is able to convince not half or three quarters but essentially all of his or her students to do quality work in school. This means to work up to their capacity, not to "lean on their shovels" as so many are doing now. All the measures of school failure that are widely reported—for example, dropout rates, low test scores, and the refusal to take hard subjects like math and science—are the result of students failing to expend the effort to do quality work. The few teachers who can consistently persuade almost all their students to do quality work are, without doubt, succeeding at the hardest job there is.

In order to explain why effective teaching is such a hard job, first I must briefly discuss work in general. I think it is safe to say that almost all work falls into one of two major categories: managing things or managing people.

When we manage things, the essence of the job is to perform an operation on a thing or even on a person (who may be acting as passively as a thing) that improves its value. What is characteristic of a thing (or a person behaving like a thing) is that, hard as the operation may be, the thing never actively resists the person managing it. Diamond cutting, for example, requires great skill but the diamond never resists the cutter. It is passive, having no agenda of its own. A medical patient and a person sitting in a hairdresser's chair are by choice more like things than people in that they resist neither the doctor nor the hairdresser. In fact, they usually try to help the person working on them to do whatever he or she is trying to do.

Jobs in which things are managed—such as carpenter,

postal worker, computer programmer, musician, truck driver, architect, and even surgeon—are in some sense much easier than jobs managing people. It is helpful if a musician has a good piano, a programmer a good computer, a truck driver a good truck, an architect good drafting tools, and a surgeon a good patient, but it is not essential. Depending upon their skills and the amount of energy they are willing to expend, they can do their jobs and be judged by others as doing it well even if the things they work on or with are flawed or the people they are trying to improve are less than cooperative. When we manage things, which have no personal agenda, we are much more in control of what we do than when we manage people. It is the well-defined, impersonal, consistent skills of the thing manager that are central to the job. For example, most skillful cabinetmakers work the wood in very much the same way.

This control makes managing things, no matter how much skill or creativity is required, much easier than managing people. Regardless of the skill and creativity of the manager, managing people depends for its ultimate success on the cooperation of the people being managed. The less the people being managed are willing to do as the manager says, the harder the job of managing them is. Teachers are people managers, and most everyone will agree that students as workers seem to be most resistant of all to being managed.

While managing workers or students to increase the quality of their work is less well defined than managing things, there is still great similarity between the skills used by effective managers of both kinds. If teachers become well acquainted with choice theory, which explains that all of our behavior is an attempt to satisfy basic needs like love and power, effective management skills will not be hard to learn. For example, while students may appear to be very different from each other, they are all driven by the same needs. The teacher who understands this will focus a great deal of effort on managing in a way that the students can satisfy their needs by doing schoolwork. When they do, and in the process discover that it is in their best interest to do quality work, the teacher's needs are satisfied also.

A graphic example of both the workers and the manager satisfying their needs was seen in a recent America's Cup competition: The crew of the winning boat and the skipper, Dennis Connor, had exactly the same need-satisfying agenda—to win. The crew followed Connor's orders without question from start to finish of each race and were overjoyed when they won. While I am sure there are a few similar examples, blind obedience is by far the exception, not the rule, when it comes to managing the vast majority of workers.

With the exception of teachers, most managers manage workers who, unless they are seriously underpaid, accept that what they are asked to do is reasonably need-satisfying. Unlike students, if they did not want to do what they were told, they would not take the job in the first place or, if they take the job anyway, they will either quit or the manager will fire them. Of course, many dissatisfied students do quit or are thrown out of school, but not before they have attended for a long time, resisting teachers every inch of the way. Other workers who do not like their jobs do not usually last as long.

There are some exceptions to the general rule that most managers deal with workers who are fairly cooperative. For example, a small number of people hold on to jobs they hate and often do poor work because they do not know how to get a better job. This is especially common when their jobs are protected by civil service rules or unions. The major exception to the rule that most workers are fairly cooperative is in the classroom. Here we have teachers and administrators trying to manage huge numbers of students who actively and passively resist what they are asked to do. From the superintendent down, all school managing is difficult, but teaching—the daily face-to-face managing of many resistant students—is not only the hardest job in the school, it is the hardest job there is.

To clarify what I mean, let me compare effective teaching with practicing medicine. Medicine is generally thought to be a very exacting profession and, for that reason, physicians are rigorously and thoroughly trained, more so than are teachers. And when physicians work, they are assisted by a variety of highly skilled and often well-paid professionals and technicians. Most physicians work in the finest workplaces that money can buy, are better compensated for what they do than all other professionals, and are treated with respect by all segments of the community. Obviously, physicians labor under far better working conditions than do teachers, and good working conditions, like good training, make any hard job easier.

But what makes medicine so much easier than teaching is more than training, pay, and working conditions. Even if teachers had better working conditions, they would still have to struggle with students who are much more resistant than patients. Patients are usually cooperative because, unlike the way many students view teachers, they almost always see their doctors as need-satisfying people. And if, as rarely happens, patients are not cooperative, few fault the doctor for refusing to treat them. Doctors, therefore, are much more in control of what they are allowed to do than teachers, and the more in control a person is, the easier that person will perceive the job.

Another integral part of what makes a job hard is how much a manager is subject to blame for doing a poor job. Those whose job it is to manage things are usually clearly at fault and quickly blamed when they do a poor job. For example, a truck driver who runs out of gas or a plumber who fails to fix a leak is quickly blamed for this obvious failure.

But it is almost always in the power of such managers to do a good job. Those who manage things, much more than those who manage people, are in control of what they do. This means that although they are clearly subject to blame when they do a poor job, they can almost always avoid blame if they make the effort to do a good job.

On the other hand, those who manage people are less obviously at fault when the people they manage do a poor job. For a long time, the tendency has been to blame the worker more than the manager. A poor student or even several poor students tend to be blamed more than their teachers. But as we are now inundated with students doing badly in school, more and more teachers, who do not believe they are at fault, are being blamed for what they do not know how to correct or being blamed for what they cannot correct because they themselves are managed badly by administrators above them. Being blamed for what you cannot correct or do not believe you can correct is extremely frustrating.

This does not mean that people managers, even administrators and some teachers, should not be held responsible when those they manage do not perform. The thrust of this book is that through better management and the move to quality education, it is possible to teach much more effectively than many teachers do now. However, the point I am trying to make here is that when a teacher is blamed for what he or she believes is almost impossible to do—for example, teach the academically unmotivated student—the teacher perceives this blame as unfair, and this makes the job especially hard.

Another factor that makes teaching such a hard job is the lack of adequate pay for such hard work. If we accept the fact that we need many more effective teachers, we also have to face the fact that a large part of what makes a job easy or hard is the pay. Digging ditches at twenty-five dollars an hour isn't easy, but it's a lot easier than it would be at five dollars an hour. Teaching will never be a high-paying job, but low pay makes it much harder than it needs to be.

Teaching also is hard because there is no relationship between how effectively a teacher teaches and the pay he or she receives for doing it. There is, therefore, no direct financial incentive for expending the time and energy needed to do this hard job better. A good argument against giving teachers a financial incentive for performance is that there is no way yet to measure performance that teachers themselves will agree is fair. For example, a teacher may do a good job all year and sell her class on the value of quality work, but the payoff of her hard work may not be obvious until the following year, when her former students buckle down.

Any system of rewards that is perceived by the workers as unfair will create bitterness and resentment. This is already a problem with merit pay and in the mentor-teacher system, and the more pay is based on arbitrary criteria, the more this problem will grow. It is not an insoluble problem, however. At the end of this book, I offer a solution for increased pay for increased performance that I believe most teachers will consider fair.

Another factor that makes effective public school teaching in this country much harder, as compared to other countries, is that we do not have the strong cultural support of education that is taken for granted in countries like Korea, Japan, France, and Germany. We have a wide variety of subcultures, many of which do not value the education offered in our schools. If they do value it, they do not value the way it is offered. While it may be overstating the case to say that some of our subcultures are anti-intellectual, we certainly have many families in which what is commonly referred to as "book learning" is not highly prized.

Even our colleges are publicized more for athletics than for academics. We take pride in the fact that someone who did not do well in school or who had little schooling—the so-called self-made man or woman—can go far in our society. A person running for high office with a Ph.D. might find it to be as great a handicap as a moral indiscretion. This ethos may be democratic and less elitist than foreign cultures, but it does not help our teachers. They have a much harder job than teachers in some foreign countries because foreign students are much more likely to be persuaded by their families to work hard in school and to do as the teacher says.

Obviously, the less resistant the students, the easier the teacher's job. It would seem, therefore, that those in the state departments of education, who are at the top of the school management hierarchy, would do all they could do to create curricula that students would not resist. But as Professor Linda McNeil points out (and supported by the rebellious West High Students described in Chapter One) this is hardly the case.[1]

Instead, as students' "achievement" is more and more being called into question by the public and has become a political issue, state after state is "measuring" achievement on the basis of "objective" tests and finding the scores too low. Driven by the fear that they will be blamed for these low scores and their power will thereby be threatened, most state departments are desperately introducing teaching "reforms" that are directly (and, I believe, blindly) aimed at raising test scores.

As Professor McNeil's research clearly shows, teachers are being asked more and more to objectify and standardize their teaching. As they do, education is being fragmented and mystified, and large areas that might in any way be controversial, and therefore interesting, such as the Vietnam War, are being omitted. As this happens, the result from the teachers' point of view is that they are more and more being treated as nonintellectual "things" and less and less as capable professionals. McNeil writes:

> Such reforms render teaching and the curriculum inauthentic. If we are to engage students in learning, we must reverse this process. When school knowledge is not credible to students, they opt out and decide to wait until "later" to learn "what you really need to know." Mechanical teaching processes knowledge in a way that guarantees it will be something other than credible. Centralized curriculum, centralized tests of outcomes, and standardized teacher behaviors can only frustrate those teachers whose passion for teaching has shown students (and the rest of us) what education should be about.[2]

To conform to this new and widespread concern that all that is taught be measured, teachers, as the managers of students, are required to turn their backs on a basic choice theory axiom: For workers, including students, to do quality work, they must be managed in a way that convinces them that the work they are asked to do satisfies their needs. The more it does, the harder they will work.

Instead, teachers are required to stuff students with fragments of measurable knowledge as if the students had no needs—almost as if they were things. Education is defined as how many fragments of information these "student-things" can retain long enough to be measured on standardized achievement tests. Most competent teachers recognize, however, that this approach has little or nothing to do with what they consider quality education, but their input is either ignored or depreciated by the politically motivated standardizers and fragment measurers who are now in charge.

Because this low-quality, standardized, fragmented approach is so unsatisfying to students (and teachers), more and more students are actively resisting and this resistance is seen as a discipline problem. School administrators then fall into the trap of thinking that discipline problems, not unsatisfying education, are the cause of low levels of achievement. This explains the increased emphasis on strict rules of deportment (more coercion), which further define a good student as a passive thing rather than an involved, questioning, even at times dissenting learner.

When this happens, as Professor McNeil found at a school she studied,

> Any deviations from administrative directives for maintaining order were dealt with by school discipline policies that frequently did not punish offenders directly but punished all students together. Both teachers and students felt herded. Many attempts to control behavior were so disproportionate to the offense that they seemed to be acts of desperation and, in turn, made students rebel in such petty ways as littering in the halls and cafeteria.[3]

Teaching is difficult under the best educational conditions, and this failure to take into account the needs of students or teachers makes what is already a hard job almost impossible. Any method of teaching that ignores the needs of teachers or students is bound to fail. Most of us are now well aware that we are increasingly paying the price for that failure in the increased use of drugs, more delinquency, and greater numbers of teenage pregnancies—to cite some of the more obvious problems.

Teachers, who must manage better than all other managers if they are to succeed at all, are being asked to accept educational working conditions that almost ensure that they will fail to persuade at least half, and usually more, of their students to do even low-quality work. For the competent teacher, it has become a miserable Catch-22: If I teach conceptually and challenge them to think and defend their ideas, which is the way I know is right, my students have a chance to succeed in learning something worthwhile, but they may not do well on the tests that measure fragments and I will be labeled a troublemaker and a failure. On the other hand, if I teach the way I am told, my students will fail to learn anything that I, and most of them, believe is worthwhile, but I will be praised as a successful team player and they will be blamed as incompetent.

Caught in this trap, many teachers are giving up on what they believe and accepting the political view that students should be treated as things and stuffed with fragments of knowledge. To teach this way, they emphasize facts and "right" answers, avoid controversy and discussion, give a great deal of homework, test frequently, and tailor what they teach to state testing programs. In doing so, they become much more impersonal than they would like and teach less of what their students want to learn than they feel is right. Nothing makes a job harder than feeling that you have to give up on what you believe.

There are probably other obstacles to overcome if we are to make the switch from boss- to lead-managing. But if we can overcome this one, we have a good chance of overcoming others. If we continue to take the skill and art of teaching lightly, believing that almost anyone can do it, and end most formal training when teachers start to teach, we will not make progress. Teaching is a very hard job that needs ample compensation and considerable on-the-job training for the lifetime of the teacher. Less than this will not suffice.

CHAPTER THREE

We Need Noncoercive Lead-Management from the State Superintendent to the Teacher

Having seen that teaching is perhaps the most difficult of all management jobs, we are now ready to take a detailed look at the crucial factor in educational reform: replacing boss-management with lead-management so that we can begin the move to quality. Boss-management is wrong because it limits both the quality of the work and the productivity of the worker. And further, as I will explain shortly, its use actually produces most of the discipline problems we are trying to prevent.

In education, where it is used almost exclusively, boss-management has effectively limited the number of students who do acceptable work (many less do quality work) to about 50 percent in the best neighborhoods and up to 90 percent in schools where there is little support for learning in students' homes. Therefore, given the hardest of management jobs, teachers as well as administrators are burdened with a method of management that limits their ability to succeed no matter how competent they are in other respects.

Boss-management is not complicated. Reduced to its essentials, it contains four basic elements:

1. The boss sets the task and the standards for what the workers (students) are to do, usually without consulting the workers. Bosses do not compromise; the worker has to adjust to the job as the boss defines it.
2. The boss usually tells, rather than shows, the workers how the work is to be done and rarely asks for their input as to how it might possibly be done better.
3. The boss, or someone the boss designates, inspects (or grades) the work. Because the boss does not involve the workers in this evaluation, they tend to settle for just enough quality to get by.
4. When workers resist, the boss uses coercion (usually punishment) almost exclusively to try to make them do as they are told and, in so doing, creates a workplace in which the workers and manager are adversaries.

Viewed as a whole, it is obvious that boss-management is much more concerned with the needs of the boss than of the workers. Because this is so obvious, many bosses have been able to see that boss-management is counterproductive. There is now some softening of this hard line, mostly in high-tech and service industries where the educational and persuasive skills of the worker are paramount to the success of the company. Schools, however, are one of the few "industries" in which boss-management is used pretty much as outlined above.

The most obvious reason for the overwhelming preponderance of boss-managers is tradition. It is "natural" for the strong to try to dominate the weak, and students are always younger and less knowledgeable (therefore weaker) than the teacher. Administrators, especially, tend to see students as subordinates, a situation tailor-made for the boss-management approach. And since schools have always been boss-managed, most teachers and administrators do not question what they do and are not even aware that a better, noncoercive method of management exists.

In industry, we now have extensive research to prove that boss-management is much less effective than lead-management,[1] but this research has had little effect on much of industry and almost no effect on the schools. I believe there are two reasons for this, both of which I address in this book:

1. Managers do not know choice theory and do not know why lead-management works. They therefore tend to distrust it even when they see it working.
2. Managers do not realize that what Deming has taught and demonstrated is that quality is the key to increased productivity.

There is always the fear, especially in education among the measurers and fragmenters who prevail at the top, that if we are too concerned with quality, students will cover less ground. Deming has shown that the opposite occurs: Quality always leads to increased productivity. Many people do not believe this because what Deming has accomplished is so contrary to "common sense."

Boss-management is also difficult to challenge because in most schools there are enough students willing to work that any teacher can say, "Look at all the students who are doing well because they are doing what they are told." But the success of these students is not due to the way they are managed: It is because of the homes they come from. It occurs despite how they are managed: If boss-management were effective, many more students would be successful.

The get-tough, coercive boss approach is the main way in which schools deal with problem students. The persuasive, lead-management approach is not known well enough even to be considered. But even if teachers were aware of this approach, they would be leery of it because they fear it lacks control. Boss-managers are not comfortable with the idea of giving up the control they believe is inherent in their traditional boss approach.

But as much as boss-management promises control, in schools it totally fails to deliver on this promise. There is no shortage of students in most schools who neither work nor follow rules. Teachers who become frustrated by these resistant students tend to request sanctions like detention, suspension, and corporal punishment, but as they use these, they become more boss-like and less effective. They fail to recognize that many students have become hardened to these limited sanctions and have no fear of them. From the students' standpoint, the need-frustrating pain of memorizing low-quality fragments is as great or greater than the pain of whatever sanction they might suffer at the hands of the teacher.

What teachers also fail to see is that these very sanctions stand in the way of achieving the quality that is essential to a highly productive workplace. This is because as soon as a boss uses coercion, especially punishment, the boss and the worker become adversaries. There is no way to keep this from happening. And while people will work for an adversary (huge numbers do and some even work hard), they do so because of their own needs. The boss is ignored, avoided, disliked, or ridiculed and is seen as either unnecessary or as an obstacle to getting the job done.

In such an atmosphere, which prevails in many work situations (schools have no monopoly here), workers will work, but very few will consistently do the high-quality work of which they are capable. Too often, work becomes a wasteful contest. The boss tries to get as much from the workers as possible while giving as little as possible, and the workers give as little as possible and still try to get what they want. This contest uses up a great deal of energy that could be better channeled into productivity and quality.

In school, the adversarial teacher-student relationship that is destructive to quality starts quickly. As early as first grade, any child who does not do as the teacher says is almost always boss-managed, and the coercion starts. It does not make much difference whether it is done subtly or overtly: The child knows when he or she is being coerced. As soon as this occurs, the child's main agenda becomes resistance, the personal power struggle between teacher and pupil begins, and education is left behind. It becomes a vicious cycle: The child learns less and resists more; the teacher coerces more and teaches less. For many children this adversarial relationship is in place by elementary school, and their formal education becomes secondary to a never-ending power struggle in which all involved are losers.

Teachers in elementary schools, however, are much less likely to use boss-management destructively than in the secondary school. The "keep-quiet-and-do-what-you-are-told" boss approach flowers in the higher grades, where teachers are pressured to "produce" and where, with well over a hundred students each day, they have little opportunity to get to know their students personally. By the end of the seventh grade, more than half the students believe that teachers and principals are their adversaries. Quality education thus becomes unavailable except to the dwindling minority who are willing to fit into the boss-defined system. Believing, correctly in most cases, that the system will never adjust to what they want or even try to find out what that is, many students drop out altogether, many more than are reported because our present statistics do not include substantial numbers of middle school dropouts.[2]

Boss-management works better if the boss uses rewards instead of punishment. Even though control remains in the hands of the boss, this tends to reduce the adversarial atmosphere that is the hallmark of boss-management. Schools, however, are largely unable to reward students, so that the best part of boss-management is mostly unavailable to students. There are, for example, no immediate rewards comparable to those in industry, such as pay increases, help from subordinates, promotions, better offices, good parking, and time off.

Even good grades, essentially the only tangible school reward, are far from immediate. Most schools depend on hazy, long-term rewards, such as the promise that students will get into a good college and get a good job if they work hard and get good grades. This is probably true, but these goals are so far in the future that fewer than half of the capable students are willing to work hard now to achieve them. Young people, especially, will not work hard for distant rewards. If they are to put out a lot of effort, they want an immediate payoff.

Therefore, it is almost impossible to coerce students to work hard enough to do quality work when they see school as nonsatisfying. What is needed instead of coercion is a great deal of creativity and patience, both of which tend to be in short supply. This does not mean that all boss-management is ineffective, but it is least effective where workers do not see the job as satisfying. It is most effective where workers and the boss have the same agendas and where the boss uses rewards more than punishment, a situation more prevalent in elementary school than in secondary school.

While boss-management is ineffective at all levels, the higher the level at which it is employed, the more damage it does to the quality of the work and the productivity of the worker. For example, teachers who use boss-management exclusively will limit the learning in their classes. A principal who is a dedicated boss-manager will make it so hard for teachers to use lead-management that the whole school will be negatively affected. A superintendent following this philosophy will cast a shadow on the whole district, and when boss-management is the philosophy in the state office, as it is in the many states that are now demanding that standardized fragments of learning be measured, the whole state will suffer.

As Deming says, "The goal is clear. The productivity of our systems must be increased. The key to change is the understanding of our managers, and the people to whom they report, about what it means to be a good manager."

LEAD-MANAGEMENT IS THE BASIC REFORM WE NEED

In contrast to the coercive core of boss-management, persuasion and problem solving are central to the philosophy of lead-management. The lead-manager spends all his time and energy figuring out how to run the system so that workers will see that it is to their benefit to do quality work. In Deming's words:

1. A manager is responsible for consistency of purpose and continuity to the organization. The manager is solely responsible to see that there is a future for the

workers. [It is our responsibility as a society to manage our schools so that almost all students get a high-quality education.]
2. The workers work in a system. The manager should work on the system to see that it produces the highest quality product at the lowest possible cost. The distinction is crucial. They work *in* the system; the manager works *on* the system. No one else is responsible for the system as a whole and improving it.[3] [This means that the administrators, much more than the teachers, are responsible for improving the system.]

Keeping these points in mind, following are the four essential elements of lead-managing:

1. The leader engages the workers in a discussion of the quality of the work to be done and the time needed to do it so that they have a chance to add their input. The leader makes a constant effort to fit the job to the skills and the needs of the workers.
2. The leader (or a worker designated by the leader) shows or models the job so that the worker who is to perform the job can see exactly what the manager expects. At the same time, the workers are continually asked for their input as to what they believe may be a better way.
3. The leader asks the workers to inspect or evaluate their own work for quality, with the understanding that the leader accepts that they know a great deal about how to produce high-quality work and will therefore listen to what they say.
4. The leader is a facilitator in that he shows the workers that he has done everything possible to provide them with the best tools and workplace as well as a noncoercive, nonadversarial atmosphere in which to do the job.

To demonstrate how these elements would work in practice, let me apply them to the teaching of algebra, a subject that many students are having difficulty learning in our predominantly boss-managed math classes. In these classes a boss-teacher sets the agenda, and the students have no say in this process. The students pass the course if the first time they take the test they are able to achieve a minimum score; even low-quality D work is passing. Large numbers of students are failing, however, because they do not do even this much or cannot do it on the only test given.

In contrast, a lead-teacher would start by discussing algebra, defining it, and explaining why it is taught and how the students could use it in their lives. If available, a videotape would be shown in which successful people from various cultural backgrounds explain how they use algebra in their lives and why it was worthwhile for them to learn it. The lead-teacher would tell the class that any student who makes an effort can learn algebra well.

After answering students' immediate questions, the teacher would then explain that much of the work would be done in small cooperative groups (a very need-satisfying way to teach) in which students would help each other. The teacher would try to assign at least one capable student to each cooperative group and would teach these student leaders how to model the problem-solving techniques for the rest of the group. The teacher would emphasize that the purpose of the groups is to help them all to understand algebra, not just to get the problems done. Schools would make an effort to train all the teachers who use cooperative learning to use it well.

The teacher would ask for students' input as to when they are ready to take the tests, based on their results on practice tests that would always precede the real exams. Students who did well on the tests would go on; students

who did not do well would then have the chance to continue working on the tested material until they mastered it.
Competency and quality would be the rule: Time would
never be a factor. The ideal of a quality school would be
that no student willing to do the work would need to be
concerned about running out of the time needed to learn.
This would mean that no one would be asked to go on to
new material until he or she had demonstrated a good
understanding of what had been covered so far.

In practice, this approach would present difficulties.
How would a teacher handle faster and slower students in
the same classroom? What we do now is to let the slower
students struggle. They either fail or end up doing work of
very low quality, hardly a sensible solution to this problem.
Or they drop algebra, enroll in general math, and never
learn higher mathematics. My solution is to find out early
who is not able to keep up in the standard one-year course
and offer a two-year course concurrently into which these
slower students could transfer. While some of the one-year
students might do higher-quality work than the two-year
students, quality would also be maintained in the slower
course. The difference would be less in the quality of the
work than in the time to do it.

In the two-year course, all students who worked would
be given sufficient time to complete each unit of the course
with competence. As they did, they would gain confidence
and begin to work a little faster, and many would go on to
higher math. (At present, students who fall behind lose
confidence and simply give up.) Students from the one-
year course could transfer into the two-year course at spec-
ified intervals during the year, knowing that the same quality standards would apply. This might mean that the faster
students would have a chance for an additional elective, or
they could be enlisted to help tutor the slower students
both in and out of class. Given a chance to teach, they

would improve their already high-quality skills. An added incentive to do this would be the chance to earn the A+ grade that I will explain in Chapter Eight. In this way, almost all who are willing to try would eventually learn to do quality algebra. And using the approach described here, many more than now would be willing to try.

From the beginning, all students, both as individuals and as a group, would be asked to evaluate the quality of their classwork, homework, and tests and to put this evaluation at the top of all they do. How they would do this would be discussed and agreed on as part of the continual give-and-take that would take place in a lead-managed class. Following Deming, the emphasis would be on involving the students in the evaluation of their own work for quality, and they would be encouraged to keep their own quality record so that they would always know exactly where they were.

The lead-teacher's job would be to facilitate continually, which would mean talking to students and listening to their input on how to keep the classroom a good place to learn and how to make improvements. Once the students discovered that they could actually do quality work in algebra, they would find a satisfaction with math that almost no students get now in their boss-managed classes. It is only the discovery that "I can do quality work" that leads to motivation, a subject I will discuss in detail in the next chapter. There would be no coercion and, therefore, no discipline problems, as they do not occur in a noncoercive atmosphere.

When the above principles are put into practice in school or elsewhere, the worker cannot help but see that the manager is as concerned with the workers' needs as with his or her own. And when the workers are students, they realize that the person they are working for is a teacher, not a boss. This is why lead-managing is so applicable to education: The very definition of good teaching is embodied in the four elements of lead-management.

While in theory the basic tactics of the two types of managers differ markedly, in practice boss-managers are rarely all boss. Few boss-managers approach their job with the coercive zeal of a marine drill sergeant, and even a drill sergeant will at times use some persuasion. On the other hand, lead-managers may be tempted to blend a little coercion into their basic lead approach, but, if they do, they risk losing their effectiveness. For this reason, the best lead-managers make a constant effort never to coerce. Even a little coercion will taint the lead atmosphere and render it adversarial because the manager will be seen as a phony. It takes a long time to persuade workers who have been boss-managed to accept that they can work in a problem-solving, give-and-take atmosphere free of coercion. If there is any coercion at all, this acceptance time is greatly extended.

This does not mean, however, that the lead-manager does nothing if a worker fails to put forth effort or breaks the rules of the workplace. There is much the lead-manager can and should do: His skill is doing it without coercion. How a teacher or administrator can accomplish this will be explained in detail in the final chapters of this book, but basically, when there is a dispute between the leader and the worker, the leader makes it clear to the worker that this is a problem they can solve together. The leader emphasizes that problems are never solved by coercion: They are solved by all parties to the problem figuring out a better way that is acceptable to all. If the first solution does not work, the problem is addressed again. Coercion is never an option, so it is almost impossible for the leader and the workers to become adversaries.

While being an effective leader may initially take more time and effort than bossing, in the end it takes much less time and effort because workers find that when they are managed by a leader, quality work is very satisfying. It is certainly possible to learn how to be an effective lead-teacher, but few teachers will make the effort to do so unless they themselves experience the benefit of this approach. This means that lead-management and the concepts of quality will not flourish in our classrooms unless they are implemented at the level of the school principal. He or she is the crucial element in educational reform.

The principal who wants to be a successful lead-manager must learn the social and administrative skills needed to be a buffer between the bosses above and the teachers he or she lead-manages. It would be good if these ideas were accepted at levels above the principal, and I am sure that this will be the case at times. But once we leave the school, the central office power struggles of educational politics almost always intrude. Bossing and kowtowing are so deeply ingrained at the top of the system that my hope for educational reform is to find enough principals willing to give up bossing and start leading.

Boss-management has failed and will continue to fail because it is not based on how we function. The following chapters present a choice theory explanation of how we function that shows clearly why lead-management and the quality ideas of W. Edwards Deming work. If this explanation makes sense to you, then maybe together we can begin to make the changes that are needed.

AN IMPORTANT WORD ABOUT STYLE

I have stated that lead-managers are not coercive, but most of us remember great teachers whose style seemed to go against this tenet. Jaime Escalante, the calculus teacher in the movie *Stand and Deliver*, seemed the antithesis of the lead-teacher: he threatened, cajoled, cursed, ridiculed, graded almost capriciously, threw students out of class, put down their interest in other activities such as playing in the band, gave huge amounts of homework, and worked students to the point of exhaustion. A few rebelled, but most revered him and accepted that what he did was for their own good.

What we must realize is that there is a very fine distinction between coercion, which is never caring, and a coercive style of teaching that is, at its core, very caring. If the workers see the manager as caring, then they can accept whatever he does, no matter how coercive it may seem on the surface. To workers, caring means that they believe their welfare is more important to the manager than either his welfare or the welfare of those above him in the organization. Further, they see the manager as desperate, not vindictive. They know that they are not used to doing quality work and that he is only attempting to get them to work harder than most have ever worked before. But they will not see this if they do not also see that the manager himself is working harder than they are used to seeing managers work. The message must come across loud and clear from the manager: No matter how hard I ask you to work, I work as hard or harder.

Therefore, the essence of good managing is caring and hard work. Acting, posturing, dramatizing, shouting, gesturing, and criticizing are styles a manager may choose as he or she attempts to add drama and excitement to what can easily become a boring process. As long as the essence is preserved, any style is within the confines of lead-management. Great leaders all have a style that works for them, and I doubt that it can (or should) be taught or even successfully imitated. It is their unique, creative approach to the difficult problem of persuading people to do what they are reluctant to do.

I believe, however, that the majority of great teachers do not use the coercive style that Escalante used so successfully. When you study great teachers, as I hope you will have a chance to do, you will learn much more from their caring and hard work than from their style. To be a successful lead-manager, you will have to develop your own style; it is the only style that will work for you.

CHAPTER FOUR

Choice Theory and Motivation

In school, boss-management is a major reason why so few students are involved in high-quality honors or advanced-placement classes. And as long as boss-managers prevail, there is little chance we will ever be able to increase this small number because boss-managers totally misunderstand what has become one of the most common management buzzwords: motivation. Boss-managers firmly believe that people can be motivated from the outside: They fail to understand that all of our motivation comes from within ourselves.

Boss-teachers and administrators constantly lament that students are not motivated, but what they are actually saying is that they do not know how to persuade students to work. And as long as they continue to believe in coercion, they never will. When it comes to understanding motivation, boss-managers are looking for something that does not exist. But they keep looking because they, like almost everyone else, accept the external control theory. According to this theory, our behavior is almost always motivated by a stimulus that exists outside of ourselves.

For example, most people believe that students stop talking because the teacher asks for silence or that jail sentences deter crime. But choice theory points out that this is not the case. Students keep quiet only when they believe it is to their benefit to do as the teacher asks; otherwise they keep talking. And our jails are filled with lawbreakers who have been there before and have not been deterred by that experience.

It is always what we want at the time that causes our behavior. The outside event (stimulus) may seem to be the cause, but it never is. Some students do not stop talking when the teacher asks; short of applying force (gagging them or dragging them from class), there is nothing any teacher can do to make them. Boss-teachers tell students every day to work hard; even though they are punished, many students still do not work hard. In fact, many do even less after they are punished. This fact does not faze boss-teachers; they continue to believe they can make students do what they are told, if only they can figure out a firmer way to tell them. One indication of this is that more teachers than the general public (56 percent compared to 50 percent) believe that they should have the right to spank children.[1]

A friend of mine stopped believing in external motivation when he was held up at gunpoint and found himself refusing to give the gunman his wallet because he did not want to lose his driver's license and credit cards. He was amazed that he ignored one of the most powerful stimuli of all, a gun. We can argue that he is lucky to be alive, but the fact is that the gunman, a firm believer in boss-management, did not get the wallet. Even a gun does not always make you boss.

This does not mean that people threatened with a gun do not usually do as they are told: Most of the time they do. But the reason they do is not just because of the threat. It is because they decide that, all things considered, it will be better for them at the time not to resist. But they resent being threatened and will do only the bare minimum of what is asked. Managers can count on coercion to achieve only the simplest tasks: Resentful workers will not do anything well that is the least bit complicated.

The same goes for reward: It is not the reward but the person's evaluation of how much he or she wants the reward that determines behavior. Managers who use rewards achieve more than managers who use punishment because rewards tend to be more need-satisfying, but workers may still resent the manager's power to give or withhold the reward. They may challenge that power by not doing as much as the manager wants, even at the risk of losing the reward altogether.

I am not saying that what happens outside of us means nothing, far from it. What happens outside of us has a lot to do with what we choose to do, but the outside event does not cause our behavior. What we get, and all we ever get, from the outside is information; how we choose to act on this information is up to us. Therefore, the information that the students get from the teacher, which includes how this information is given, is very important. In fact, this whole book is about its importance. But the students are the ones who make the ultimate judgment about how important it is to them. The more important they think it is, the more they will do what they are asked and the better they will do it.

If I point a gun at you and ask for your wallet, that whole sequence for you is information. You will do, and only do, what you think is best. Most of you will give up your wallets because you decide your life is more important than your wallet, but some of you, like my friend, will not. The difference between a lead-manager and a boss-manager is in the information each gives to the worker or student, and this is a huge difference. In practice, it is the main difference between students working or "leaning on their shovels." The message from the boss-manager is always coercive, be it reward or punishment, because the bosses think that this is the best way to "motivate" workers. Bosses like to point guns more than they like to raise salaries and are always looking for bigger guns. Effective lead-managers never use coercive messages but instead try to give the workers the kind of information that will persuade them to do as they are directed because it is as much or more to their benefit as it is to the manager's.

But if they know choice theory, lead-managers also know what information that we, as humans, are always looking for. Using this knowledge, an effective lead-manager makes an effort to combine what workers are looking for (actually what all humans are looking for) with what he or she is asking them to do. If the manager succeeds, it is very likely that the workers will decide not only to do the work but to do it well.

When boss-teachers complain that nothing they do seems to motivate students to work hard, what they are really saying is that they have not succeeded in giving these students the right message. Given the usual coercive messages, "unmotivated" students ignore them and choose not to work. But the fact that students choose not to do schoolwork does not mean they lack motivation: No human being is unmotivated. In fact, every living creature is highly motivated all the time. Students are no exception to the choice theory axiom that all living creatures are always motivated by the basic needs of their species. But every living creature, including students, is not necessarily motivated to do what you, I, or anyone else thinks they ought to do. There is certainly no basic need to do schoolwork.

If, however, what we are asked to do also satisfies one or more of our basic needs, a great deal of work gets done. If we care for the manager, we may even do what is distasteful to us because pleasing the manager strongly satisfies our basic need for love and friendship. This means that as much as we dislike it, we may learn grammar because we care for the teacher who teaches it. But if we stop caring for this teacher, we may stop learning grammar. Students will do things for a teacher they care for that they would not consider doing for a teacher they did not care for.

But there is a limit to what we will do for someone we care for if it is distasteful to us. In fact, much misery is caused by our failure to understand that we cannot get other people, even if we love them and they love us, to do what we want them to do if it is extremely unsatisfying to them. Many parents have struggled painfully to try to "make" a child they love change his or her ways because they "know" that what they want the child to do is better for that child than what the child is doing.

Time may even prove the parents right. However, when they are engaged in what is too often a losing battle, for example, when a teenager starts to stay out half the night even on school nights, the parents may worry and suffer beyond belief. But the more the parents act the boss and try to coerce the child into coming home at a reasonable hour, the less control they seem to have and the more miserable they are.

The crucial difference between boss-managers and lead-managers is mainly in how they understand motivation. Bosses refuse to accept that they cannot "motivate" the workers with what they believe will cause the workers pain or give them pleasure, especially when they also believe that what they are asking is good for the workers. Following this belief, bosses constantly look for new sanctions or rewards to "make" the workers work. Leaders, on the other hand, know that they cannot make the workers work hard if the work is seen as unsatisfying or they are seen as unconcerned about the workers' needs.

To understand what motivation actually is, it is necessary first to understand that choice theory contends that all human beings are born with five basic needs built into their genetic structure: survival, love, power, fun, and freedom. All of our lives we must attempt to live in a way that will best satisfy one or more of these needs.

Choice theory is a descriptive term because we try to control our own behavior so that what we *choose* to do is the most need-satisfying thing we can do at the time. Although we can control only our own behavior, it is obvious that much of what we choose to do is an attempt to control others. For example, many of us attempt to stop people we love from destroying themselves with addicting drugs. But to do this we can control only what *we* do. Choice theory, therefore, is the explanation of this constant attempt to control both ourselves and others, even though in practice we can control only ourselves.

Keep in mind that "control" in this context means to control as in steering a car or following a recipe. It does not mean to dominate by using force or the threat of force, as a police officer does to subdue a criminal. And although we may say, "I forced myself," we do not really use force on ourselves. What we mean is that it was particularly difficult for us to choose to do as we did.

Our genes, which in essence are the biological instructions for what we are to become, not only dictate what our structure is to be (for example, our eye color) but also (and this claim is unique to choice theory) how we, as humans, must attempt to live our lives. Just as a northern migrating bird must always attempt to fly south for the winter, we, too, must attempt to live our lives in ways that we believe will best satisfy our needs. If what we are asked to do in school does not satisfy one or more of these needs or we do not care for the teacher who asks us to do it, then we will do it poorly or even not at all.

From birth, our behavior is always our best attempt at the time to do what we believe will best satisfy one or more of our needs. We can no more deny that these needs exist and are constantly on our mind (whether we are aware of it or not), than we can deny the shape of our nose or the color of our eyes. And regardless of our cultural background, we are all members of the same species, and all of us have the same genetic needs. We spend our lives trying to learn how to satisfy these needs, but most of us do not have a clear idea of what they are, especially when we are young. What we always know, however, is how we feel. And what we actually struggle for all of our lives is to feel good. It is from our ability to feel, essentially from our ability to know whether we feel good or bad, that most of us gain some idea of what our needs are.

Because they are well able to tell the difference between pain and pleasure, newborn babies quickly learn to express themselves so that those who take care of them can tell whether they are feeling good or bad. Parents may not know exactly how to help a baby feel better, but they almost always know how the baby feels. Very quickly, babies become better at expressing what is wrong and parents become more adept at guessing what it is.

It does not take long before parents are also able to figure out how to help the baby to feel better, which is the same as saying how to help the baby satisfy his or her needs. Using the information constantly available to them about how they feel, children learn as they grow what feels good and what feels bad. As they do, they learn to satisfy their own needs or to get help from others (like their parents) if they cannot do it for themselves.

Even before starting school, most children are told by their families that school is good for them, and they expect school to feel good. And in the beginning it usually does feel good: For most children, kindergarten is a very need-satisfying experience. As they progress, however, what they do in school does not feel as good as it did in kindergarten. When they question this dropoff, they are told that what they are taught is still good for them because it will help them later. The strong implication is, "Continue working hard, but also be patient because there will be less that feels good immediately and more that will not feel good until later."

The problem is that the genetic needs themselves know nothing about later: They are continually pushing us to do what feels good now. You can tell your stomach that you are not going to feed it because you want to lose weight, but you cannot stop your stomach from telling you that it wants food right now. A measure of our strength, often called strength of character, is how much we can learn to tolerate pain or delay pleasure while doing what is "good" for us in the long run. As stated in the last chapter, if we have a supportive family and can satisfy our needs at home, getting through a frustrating day at school or work is a lot easier.

Even with strong family support, it's hard to get through many bad days. Without this support, it may be impossible. Not enough students have the strength to keep working hard if they encounter day after day of painful frustration, and many subjects, taught now in the fragmented way described in the first chapter, are miserably boring. Since we all want to suffer as little possible, many students who feel bad choose to stop working in school.

A good lead-manager is able to predict how much pain a worker will put up with in the present and still keep working hard for a future payoff. Right now school managers are making this prediction very accurately: Far too many students are refusing to work hard for what seems to be a too-distant payoff. What teachers have no way of knowing is how much family support their students have. Too many teachers mistakenly believe their students have more family support than they actually have.

This is an easy mistake to make because teachers, like all of us, tend to draw on their own experience, and most teachers had more family support when they were young than their students do. You probably did not have much use for higher math when you took it, and you were well aware that there were more enjoyable things to do than study for a math exam. But you studied anyway because you decided, based on information you got from your family, whom you believed, that this effort was necessary if you were to get some power later on. You may not have known about your need for power, but you were aware that your future might depend on doing well in math.

If you had known about your basic needs, you might have been even more willing to work and may have even been willing to work with less family support. Chapter Eleven discusses teaching students choice theory so that they might use its concepts to make better choices in their lives, especially to work hard in school and to stay away from addicting drugs. It is always helpful to know about our needs, especially our need for power, because we can use this knowledge to help us accept short-term pain when there is a good chance that this sacrifice will lead to power and long-term pleasure later.

For those in the position of managing people, knowledge of needs is more than helpful, it is essential. For example, when I present my ideas to teachers and administrators, I usually interview six junior or senior high school students in front of a large audience. Because for young people the need for power is very difficult to satisfy, I always ask, "Where in school do you feel important?" This question always seems to the students to come from outer space; they look at me as if I had asked something ridiculous. Even for the very good students, who are the group usually selected to be interviewed, feeling important (powerful) in school is an experience that few seem to think relates to them.

However, when I persist, most students tell me that they feel important in their extracurricular activities: Sports, music, and drama are most frequently mentioned. Almost never mentioned are academic classes. When asked why this is so, they say that in the extracurricular situations, where they work together as a group or on a team, they work harder and accomplish more because they help each other and have more fun. They also emphasize that they are both more comfortable and less bored in these situations because it is accepted that they socialize while they work, which is unacceptable in their regular classes. From the standpoint of choice theory, these students are saying that it is very hard for them to satisfy their needs in academic classes because most work is done alone and there is little or no class discussion.

To remedy this, I urged in *Choice Theory* (formerly *Control Theory) in the Classroom* that we teach students in cooperative groups in their academic classes. Learning as a member of a small learning team is much more need-satisfying, especially to the needs for power and belonging, than learning individually. Good lead-managers recognize that when they can promote and support worker cooperation, they have laid the foundation for quality work. Since I have already argued extensively for this approach in my earlier book, it need not be repeated in this one.

If we attempt to manage people without taking their needs into account, we will ask them to do things without considering whether or not those things are need-satisfying either now or later. Lead-managers know that the more immediately need-satisfying the work is, the harder people will work. Of course, everything we ask students to do in school cannot be immediately satisfying. But at the least, it has to lead to later satisfaction, and students need to know when and where this satisfaction will come. Lead-managers make a point to give students this information. To the extent that the work is not satisfying now or later, students will not do it and the manager will fail.

In terms of how they handle the need-satisfaction of those they manage, there is a marked difference between boss-managers and lead-managers. Boss-managers tell people what they should do and often how to do it. They also tell them that it is the best thing for them to do at the time. To the extent that they take the workers' needs into account, boss-managers imply that doing what they are told is the best way for workers to feel good (or to satisfy their needs).

Basically, the boss-teacher is not that concerned with the students' needs. This type of teacher does not work at making friends with students and sees the work as more important than the atmosphere in which it is done. Contrary to what Deming advises, the boss-teacher works on the students, not on the system. In this tense situation, where low grades abound, it is hard for all but a few students to satisfy their needs. Far too many stop trying altogether.

To be fair, boss-teachers are willing to reward workers who work hard and do well, but, as discussed in the previous chapter, except for good grades there are few rewards available that mean much to students. Whatever other rewards they use, the bosses tend to decide on them on their own and rarely try to find out from their students if these rewards are what the students want. The bosses decide what the rewards should be, and often they are not as need-satisfying to the students as the bosses believe.

Basically, boss-managers tell the workers that they know what is best for them and that they are willing to use what power they have to coerce the workers to get the work done, regardless of their needs.

While some people may have stronger needs than others, for example, some people seem to want more love or more power than others, in most cases this difference is not significant. Just as most adults are between four and seven feet tall, most of us want similar amounts of love, power, fun, and freedom, and all of us will struggle fairly hard to survive if we are in danger. For all practical purposes, there are few significant differences among us in what we need. Where we differ significantly is in how successful we are in getting it.

I think it is safe to say that some students are lucky enough to be born into homes, usually affluent, where their parents boss them less than most children are bossed. In this less coercive atmosphere, they learn more ways to satisfy their needs than those who are bossed more. Children from affluent homes not only tend to be bossed less but they also get more help from their parents as they learn to satisfy their needs. They also have the opportunity to live in better neighborhoods and to go to "better" schools. In these schools they are also bossed less than students from less affluent homes. They work harder to please their parents because they can count on more love and attention, and they and their teachers have similar academic agendas. Because of all these factors, school is more satisfying for them than it is for less affluent students. Students from affluent homes do most of the quality work that is done in public school.

For the less advantaged, boss-management both at home and in school is a double disaster: First, such students have learned fewer need-satisfying behaviors than children from advantaged homes, and they come to school both less willing and less able to do the work. They are, therefore, more easily frustrated. This means that almost from the start they do not do as well in school, even though they are inherently just as capable as the advantaged students who do better. Second, less advantaged students are bossed more than the lucky students by people who assume that this will "motivate" them to do better. In this oppressive (to them) boss atmosphere, they refuse to work even more; as they continue to be pushed and punished, they learn to hate school. Unfortunately, school for most of them is the only place outside of home where they can learn significant ways to satisfy their needs. In the end they get much less from school than they need, and many become both a burden and a danger to the society in which they live.

By late middle school or early high school, there is a state of almost total antagonism between the teachers and the nonworking students, who sometimes number as many as 90 percent of the students in schools in economically deprived neighborhoods. When such high numbers are involved, this angry atmosphere takes too much energy to maintain. Both sides tend to slip into a kind of sullen, apathetic truce: "I won't bother you if you don't bother me." This truce is fragile. When it is broken, which happens frequently when either teachers or students get excessively frustrated, anger explodes from one or both sides.

This is also the sad state of affairs for up to half the students in even our best public secondary schools. The atmosphere may be less explosive, but the sullen antagonism is just as high. And unless we eliminate the boss-management that does not address itself to the needs of students, we will stay right where we are or lose even more ground. We need to accept the fact that, right now, the majority of boss-managed students see little chance to satisfy their needs by working hard in school, and we cannot boss them into doing more.

Many teachers, however, point out that years ago "all" students worked hard because they were punished if they did not. There may be some truth in this, but it is more likely that students who did not work were punished so much that they left school or were thrown out. Because of large early dropout rates, before World War II the upper grades contained a higher percentage of students who wanted to learn than they do now.

Today, as it has become obvious to almost all families and to many students, rich or poor, that having a chance for a good life requires a diploma, more students than ever are staying in school. But staying in a school where they do not believe they can satisfy their needs means that they will not work hard or do quality work. A well-researched article on the "dropout" problem states:

> American Business is spending $30 billion a year train-ing employees in reading and math skills that they should have received in high school. . . . If the problem of school dropouts and a faltering educational system is not met head on it is not just individuals but the entire nation that is at risk, said David P. Gardner, President of the University of California System and the head of a blue-ribbon panel studying the issue. . . . "The task must be faced and the price must be paid," Gardner said. "We are out of alternatives."[2]

We have to recognize that although we cannot make stu-dents work harder, either lead-management in school or family support at home will lead to harder-working stu-dents. If both are present, the student is almost certain to do well in school. If neither is present, the student will probably be a nonachiever in school and no amount of coercion will change that. It would, of course, be wonder-ful if more families were supportive of the value of education. But what schools can and should do is manage students in a way that they can better satisfy their needs by what they do in school.

Like boss-managers, lead-managers have the goal of getting their workers to work hard, but to do this they continually keep the needs of the workers in mind. I illustrated this in Chapter Three with the description of how a hypothetical algebra teacher could persuade many more students to learn the material. I think it would be worthwhile to review that example and show how this approach relates to the basic needs. From the first day, the lead-teacher attempts to create a work situation that is warm and friendly and totally noncoercive. Students quickly realize that this teacher is not their adversary and is not trying to satisfy his or her need for power by bossing them.

As long as they are willing to work hard, the teacher will fight to protect them from others who would boss them. For example, if the students are learning but also noisy, the lead-teacher will protect them from an administrator who thinks that the only good work is quiet work. Classes may be noisy because the lead-teacher teaches in cooperative groups, and research shows that when there is a lot of interaction, often noisy, students learn more. The teacher also encourages students to work together at home as many will not do homework if they have to do it alone. In the classroom, the teacher goes from group to group and gets to know each student in a way that would not be possible simply by lecturing or assigning individual deskwork. While getting to know the students, the teacher is continually looking for a better way to teach and asking for their input on what this way might be.

The lead-teacher emphasizes that while algebra is difficult, it is far from impossible. It requires no special talent, and all who work will be able to learn it well. Both in class and in their homework, the teacher tries hard not to let students settle for anything less than getting their work correct, even if they do only one problem. But even more important than getting the problems right is understanding what they did to get them right. The emphasis is always on knowing how to do the math and where it may be applied in their lives.

The lead-teacher also explains that the only purpose of grades is to show what the students know. (Grades will be discussed extensively in Chapter Eight.) A low grade does not mean failure; it means that the student has not yet learned enough. Until the final grade, all grades are temporary: Any low grade along the way can and should be raised. By demonstrating that they know more than they did, students will get a higher grade to replace a low one. The teacher explains that he or she personally hates low grades and loves to give higher ones: All the students have to do is to be willing to do the work. The teacher thus shows that grades will be used to empower, never as a weapon or as punishment. This is in marked contrast to boss-teaching: Students often feel powerless and frustrated over grades when low grades are used punitively and never raised.

Although the emphasis is on hard work, the class atmosphere is never grim. The mood that the lead-teacher tries to create is one of enjoyment: As long as we have to work, let's have some fun along the way. Lead-managers, however, are much more willing than boss-managers to allow the workers to have a part in determining what is the best way to do the work. To accomplish this, the lead-teacher spends a small part of almost every class asking for students' input on how more can be learned or what can be done to make the class more enjoyable. The teacher does not reject the idea of rewards but believes that the class should set its own rewards if it judges that it is doing good work. Students are encouraged to plan activities both in and out of class as a reward for doing good work, and the teacher attends some of the out-of-class get-togethers as part of the commitment to the whole social process of which he or she is an important part.

The lead-teacher recognizes that the needs most satisfied by this way of teaching are for all of us the hardest to satisfy—power and belonging—and is always trying to help students satisfy these needs as they work. Lead-teachers accept what boss-teachers find hard to accept—the more power the teacher is given, the less he or she should use to boss students. The real power comes from students' perceptions of the teacher as competent to do the job, which is to show and model what is to be done and to create a good environment in which to work. Students appreciate the fact that the lead-teacher never threatens or punishes but says that if there are problems, "We will work them out." The lead-teacher's need for power is satisfied by a job well done, not by having students be subservient.

Assuming that the administrators manage teachers in the same way that I suggest teachers manage students, what has been proposed here may sound marvelous to some teachers. They may also say that I have described a pipe-dream: "No one would let me teach this way or treat me like this." What they are saying is that this kind of teaching and managing goes against the traditional boss-manager premise that seems to dominate education: Neither students nor teachers can be trusted to do what is best for them; they have to be told what to do and coerced into doing it. Therefore, even when lead-teachers get results, as they consistently will, what they do to get these results might be seen as a threat both to those who boss them and to the boss-teachers who teach alongside them.

Even if her students are working, the lead-teacher may be told that her discipline is lax because there is laughter in her class. If she is creative, as she must be to teach in a need-satisfying way, she will be told that she is deviating from the time-tested (deadly) way to plan her lessons, which is to lecture and give ditto work for students to do by themselves at their desks. One group of high-performing students told me they were being "ditto'd to death" in their high school.

The lead-teacher will also be criticized for caring too much and told that too much personal involvement is unprofessional. She will be admonished to keep the state assessment tests in mind and to fragment the subject so that students will do better on these tests, even though this approach fails to capture the attention of over half the students. She will quickly learn that in schools (as well as in a world) dominated by boss-managers, she will be unpopular for what she believes and especially for what she does. She will see many boss-teachers failing miserably, but still most of those who run the system will continue to support what the boss-teachers do as right and criticize her as wrong.

It is this kind of boss-thinking that leads to the totally destructive premise that school needs to be a struggle between the teachers (bosses) and the students (workers), and if the bosses relax even for a moment the students will destroy the school. But the sad truth is that many of our schools are already very close to being destroyed: Some of our central city schools are no longer even semblances of places of learning. The more we depend on boss-managers to solve the problem, the more we will lose of what little we have.

It is my contention that successful teachers and administrators, whether they are aware of it or not, use choice theory, which I will further explain in the two following chapters. But most teachers will not make an effort to learn choice theory unless they are firmly and warmly supported by administrators who also have become conversant with it. If teachers' attempts to become lead-managers are only tolerated, boss-management will prevail. Teachers need to be led, which means to be encouraged and praised by administrators who go into their classes and compliment both them and their students for any quality work they do. Lead-managers must actively promote need-satisfaction at all levels of the system; any less will not work.

CHAPTER FIVE

The Quality World

In the last chapter, I explained that we are all motivated by five basic needs that are built into our genetic structure. Our behavior is always our best attempt at the time to satisfy one or more of these needs. It is important to remember that even though our needs are essentially the same, the behavior we choose to satisfy them may be quite different. For example, one student may gain power by excelling in math and another by disrupting his math class. As we have seen, given the way our schools are managed, differences in family support may be the best explanation for why this happens.

While probably accurate, this explanation is of little help to the teacher who is trying to teach a disruptive student. The teacher cannot increase the support of that student's family. But understanding the disruptive student's need for power can certainly help. If the teacher can persuade the disruptive student to work hard enough to get even one good grade, the student may feel so good that he or she stops disrupting and starts to work for more good grades. Or if the teacher decides that the student is lonely and is being disruptive to get attention, the teacher may be able to assign work in a small cooperative group in which the student can get some of the desired attention.

These, however, are big "ifs." In practice, frustrated students are very difficult to manage successfully. This is because, to solve problems, most teachers depend upon coercion. This approach not only fails to work, but almost always makes the problems worse. If we cannot persuade students (without coercion) that it is to their benefit to do quality work in school, we will do nothing to improve the schools. Those who run our schools must realize that most of the problems have been caused by boss-management, and they must begin the process of changing to lead-management. Problems will then be prevented, and only through prevention will we make progress.

Take the example of seat belts: It took a long time before people accepted them as a good idea. And while we should all support medical research into the treatment of trauma, seat belts will prevent problems such as brain damage that medicine may never solve. It may take a long time for lead-management to be accepted. But, having gone as far as we can in trying to improve education through coercion, we should now turn to quality as the best way to prevent problems. To do this, however, we need to understand the choice theory concept of the quality world.

While our underlying motivation is always an attempt to satisfy one or more of the five basic needs, few of us are actively aware that these needs exist. When we are lonely and miserable, we do not complain that our need for belonging is unsatisfied: We look for a friend. When we are hungry, we do not complain that we are having difficulty surviving: We look for a meal. We look because we know we will feel good when we find what we are looking for, not because we think we have to satisfy this need or that.

As previously mentioned, what we know at birth and will know all of our lives is how we feel. It may be a while before we are actually aware of the concepts of pain and pleasure, but from the beginning we know the difference between these two basic feelings, and very quickly we learn specifically what feels good and what feels bad. Beginning shortly after birth, we learn to remember all that we do, or all that happens to us, that feels very good. We then collect these very pleasurable memories into what is best called a quality world, and this memory world becomes the most important part of our lives.

For most of us, this world is composed of pictures (or perceptions, to be more exact) and represents what we have best enjoyed in our lives. These pictures become the standards for what we would like to enjoy again and again if we could. If we attempt to manage people without knowing about the part the quality world plays in their lives, we will not be effective.

To clarify this important idea, consider a newborn baby: It will be obvious that the baby is almost helpless and will quickly die if not cared for. The baby has needs but has no idea of what they are or how to satisfy them. But she is already well aware of how she feels, and she has (or soon learns) some very primitive behaviors like screaming or cooing that help those who care for her to guess how she feels.

The baby also has senses. She does not know what they are or even what they sense, but in a minimal way she can see, hear, touch, smell, and taste. And finally, the baby has considerable capacity to learn from her behavior, minimal as this may be, that what she does may change what she senses. For example, very early in life when she feels the pangs of hunger, she learns to scream. Assuming that the baby is cared for by her mother, the mother soon figures out that the baby needs to be fed and feeds her.

As this process occurs repeatedly, the baby begins to learn that there is a relationship between her hunger pangs, her choice to scream, and the pleasure of getting fed. She also begins to sense, and then learn, that "something" out there feeds her. What she also quickly learns is that she can control the "something" out there through her screaming so that the "something" consistently does things that make her feel better.

Eventually the baby learns specifically who is out there, that this person has a name, "Mother," and that Mother helps her whenever she hurts. As this learning process continues, the baby uses all of her senses like a multisensory camera to take a picture of a loving, helping mother and stores this very satisfying picture as one of what will become her special collection of need-satisfying memories—the quality world. In this place in her memory, for the rest of her life, this child will store the most need-satisfying or quality pictures of everything she perceives. Most of us have a picture of our mother in this special world for much, if not all, of our lives.

Unlike the basic needs that are about the same for all of us, the pictures in our special world are very specific and completely individual. No two of us could possibly have the same pictures because no two of us live the same lives. It is called the quality world because it contains our best or highest-quality pictures or perceptions of the people, things, and situations that we have learned feel especially good in the real world. As we live, this special world grows, and eventually we have a collection of wonderfully satisfying pictures or perceptions in our head. If we were able to live in a real world that was exactly like this Shangri-la of our memory, life would be perfect.

Even though it is never more than a small part of our memory, this quality world is the most important part of our lives. What makes it so important is that these are the pictures we make an effort to pursue all of our lives. If something is not pictured in this quality world, we will not expend much effort pursuing it. The reason that many students do not work hard in school is that they do not have a picture of schoolwork in their quality world. Unless we can manage them so that many more are persuaded that schoolwork belongs in this world, we will not solve the problems of our schools.

When we are young, whenever we hurt, most of us will turn to the picture of our mother in our quality worlds. When we do, we immediately look for her in the real world to help us get rid of the pain. Because mother is for almost all children, and many adults, a very need-satisfying picture, we will listen carefully to what she says. In the same way, we will listen to all the other people we picture in this world. If a person is not pictured in our quality world, however, we will rarely do anything difficult that he or she may ask us to do.

Most small children come to school ready to work because people they love have told them to obey their teacher. In the beginning, the teacher may not be in the children's quality world. If what she asks them to do is not satisfying or she uses a great deal of coercion, they may never admit her. And they will pay less and less attention to what she asks them to do. Mother may get the process started, but the teacher has to get into the child's quality world to keep it going. As far as the direction of our lives is concerned, the most important pictures in our quality world are pictures of people. We will listen to and trust these quality people because we have learned that they are very much a part of why we feel good.

While we can live for years without learning exactly what our basic needs are, by age two or three we begin to suspect that there are some general conditions like love and survival that are strongly related to how we feel. When we engage in loving behaviors with people like our parents, we feel good, and when we are hungry and eat good food, we also feel good. From this it is easy to relate our parents to love and food to survival. Soon we begin to understand how important freedom is, and through laughter we quickly learn about fun even though few of us realize it is a basic need. And when people listen to us or pay attention to what we do, we feel good and begin to get the idea that we have a little power. We soon discover, however, that power is not easy to acquire. More people would rather that we listen to them than pay much attention to us. It is so hard to find power that many of us have difficulty accepting it as a need. Once we become aware of a need, we place it as a general picture in our quality world and attach it to the specific quality pictures that are very important to all of us.

It is easy to see that a need-satisfying picture may relate to all of the basic needs. From a caring, responsible mother, for example, we are better able to survive, gain love, feel powerful through her support, have fun as we laugh with her, and find the joys of freedom as she encourages us to strike out on our own. It is similar for a caring teacher or manager. A good lead-teacher may become a strong picture in our quality world because he or she teaches survival skills, becomes a good friend, shares a few laughs, and gives us freedom to learn as we see best. Where a teacher may have more difficulty than our mother is in helping us to satisfy our need for power because the teacher does not have as much time as our mother to listen to us. This means that a teacher or manager who wants to get into our quality world must continually encourage the students or the workers to express themselves and then to listen carefully to what they have to say.

It is in this area, listening, that lead-managers differ greatly from boss-managers. Lead-managers try constantly to empower the workers by listening to what they have to say. Boss-managers are less secure. They fear that if they listen too much to the workers, they will lose some of their power. By remaining aloof, they try to make sure that the

workers do not lose sight of the fact that they are in charge.
It is not that lead-managers are not ultimately in charge,
but that they avoid making their power an issue as they
manage. They try to get the workers to understand that
although they are in charge of the workplace as a whole,
their job is not so much to boss as it is to help the workers
overcome any obstacles that may stand in the way of doing
quality work. Lead-managers also make it clear to the
workers that the reason they want quality work is to make
sure that everyone has a secure, well-paid job. The foundation of successful managing is conveying the message to the
workers that the higher the quality of their work, the more
they will be in charge of their work. And because high-quality work (and certainly this includes schoolwork) leads to
economic security, they are more in charge of their lives.

Workers do not usually want to run the company, but,
driven by their needs for power and freedom, they want
some say as to how they do their work. If they do not have
any control over what they are asked to do, they feel powerless: They will not put a picture of the job or the manager
into their quality world, and they will not do quality work.
Because most students are boss-managed and do not
believe that they are important or are in charge of what
they are asked to do, they will not put either the teacher or
what is taught into their quality world.

Persuading students to do quality work is even more difficult than persuading workers to do the same. Partly this
is because workers are paid, but mostly it is because many
more workers than students are able to see the quality in
the work they are asked to do. For example, a cleaning person can more easily see the quality in a job as menial as
mopping a floor until it is spotless than a student can see
the quality of learning history or English. Although industrial managers have the job of persuading workers to
expend the effort to do quality work, they rarely have to

explain what quality is. The workers can usually recognize quality when they see it. With schoolwork, however, this does not happen as often. The quality of academic work like history, English, and math is not apparent to most students until they begin to do it. This was well brought out in *Stand and Deliver,* a movie that illustrates many of the points I am trying to make in this book.

We are usually able to recognize quality work because we have some standard quality words—for example, neat, clean, prompt, durable, shiny, functional, smooth, attractive, valuable, tasteful, competitive, polite, sensitive, thoughtful, and accurate—in our quality world. When we use any of these words to describe a job or a product, it is likely that we will see that job or product as quality. Most of these same words also describe quality schoolwork, but the connection is not nearly as clear. To help students recognize the quality of what they do, good teachers spend time and effort teaching the relationship between these standard words and the quality of the work they assign.

Lead-teachers explain what they mean by quality schoolwork and post quality papers for students to inspect. Further, to convince students that what they do has quality, a part of all assignments, both individual and group, is for the students to assess the quality of what they do. As long as the students are cautioned to avoid harsh criticism, which is almost always destructive, they might also be asked to assess the quality of the work that others do and to discuss how they came to their conclusions. It is from these discussions that students get a tangible idea of what quality is and what has to be done to achieve it.

For example, in English, a lead-teacher might first assign an essay to a student and then ask the student to assess the quality of the completed essay. The student might rate it as high quality because it is neat, no words are misspelled, and the grammar is correct. But the teacher may give the essay a lower rating because it is not written in an interesting way. Or a history student may rate a completed assignment as high quality because the dates and places are all correct, even though the student does not understand the historical reason for what happened.

The reverse may also happen. The student may hand in an essay with poor grammar and spelling, even sloppy erasures and crossouts, and give the work a high rating because the ideas are expressed creatively and with emotional impact. The teacher may downgrade the essay because of the obvious technical errors. Or a history student may know the historical significance of events but be downgraded by the teacher for not knowing the exact dates or places. Obviously, quality in schoolwork is not nearly as clear-cut as it may be on a student's after-school job.

When there is a difference between the student's and the teacher's assessment of the quality of an assignment or test, the teacher should discuss this difference with the student. From these discussions students learn to judge what determines quality work. It is also very important that students be given a chance to improve their work: If we are not going to try to improve what we do, there is little sense in assessing it. Even if the teacher and student have the same assessment, it is still worth discussing because there could be different reasons for the same assessment. Good managers do their best to teach what quality is, especially in situations where it is not obvious and schoolwork is frequently one of those situations.

In many of the schools in which I have worked, both teachers and students take for granted that most of the work will not be high quality. And as long as we do not make an effort to teach students what quality work is, this will continue. Lead-managers do not accept that students cannot do quality work, but they are aware that many students do not know what it is and have almost never done it.

They know that until a student or a worker becomes aware of what quality is and has experienced enough to find it need-satisfying, there is little chance it will be pursued with determination.

Another aspect of lead-teaching that differs from lead-managing in industry is that the teacher needs to make more of an effort than the industrial manager to get into the workers' quality world. Industrial workers are more likely than students to do quality work because they are more concerned with survival, and they are also much less dependent on the manager than students are on the teacher. For example, once most workers learn what to do, they are perfectly capable of continuing to do it well if they wish; as long as they do the job well, the manager may pay little attention except, if the manager is wise, to give an occasional compliment. On the other hand, as soon as students do something well, they go on to something new and are closely involved with the teacher in the whole process. Schoolwork changes frequently, and the quality of the teacher is as important as the quality of the work. Students will not work hard for a teacher who is not firmly embedded in their quality worlds. A teacher must expend more time and effort trying to satisfy a student than an industrial manager needs to do for a worker.

Students tell me that a good teacher is deeply interested in the students and in the material being taught. They also say that such a teacher frequently conducts class discussions and does not lecture very much. Almost all of them say that a good teacher relates to them on their level; the teacher does not place herself above them, and they are comfortable talking with her. They also tell me that a good teacher does not threaten or punish and that they have little respect for teachers who do. What they are actually saying is that these are their criteria for admitting a teacher into their quality worlds.

Students also tell me that they appreciate teachers who make an effort to be entertaining. To maintain student interest month after month in potentially boring courses, good lead-teachers try to inject humor, variety, and drama into the lessons. How to be entertaining cannot be taught: Each teacher must work it out in his or her own way, but it is another way to gain admission into students' quality worlds. While this was not mentioned in Chapter Two, the desirability that a teacher be entertaining is a further indication of how difficult it is to be an effective teacher.

Even if a teacher is willing to make the effort to be entertaining, boss-administrators tend to frown on these teachers and on their efforts. Bosses who thrive on coercion believe in the virtue of "no pain, no gain," and they do not fret if a boring teacher uses threats to keep students in line. They do not realize that boredom is the enemy of quality and that part of their jobs is to do more than encourage: It is to nurture teachers as they struggle to put fun and interest into their work. Good administrators will use humor as they deal with students and, through this model, encourage teachers to do the same.

In a good marriage, both husband and wife have satisfying pictures of each other and of their marriage in their quality worlds. Because of these pictures, they work hard to solve any problems that arise. If, however, the problems become overwhelming and the partners cannot find satisfaction in the marriage, one or both will take the picture of the other out of their quality worlds. When this happens, they divorce. They may not go through the legal process and may even continue to live together for religious, family, or economic reasons, but one or both may be miserable, and the marriage as a satisfying relationship is over.

The same thing can happen in school. Once a student takes the picture of school out of his or her quality world, the student becomes "divorced" from school. For a variety of reasons, the student may not actually leave school, but he or she will not work to get even a minimal education. Just as judges many years ago could legally force married people to stay together except when there was adultery, we can force students to stay in school. We can even try to force them to do schoolwork, but we will almost never succeed. We cannot force people to put pictures in or take pictures out of their quality worlds.

While it is possible that husbands and wives who have removed each other's pictures from their quality worlds will get back together, it rarely happens. It is also possible to persuade an alienated student to start working in school again, but this, too, rarely happens. If a "divorced" student is to get started again in school, it usually has to be in a new school, just as remarriage is usually with a new partner. Continuation schools are havens for "divorced" students. When these schools succeed, they are lead-managed. It is in these schools that we find most of the lead-management that exists in education. Boss-management has, in fact, led to the need for these alternatives.

Because students see their school as need-satisfying, there are almost no discipline problems. Even though they are doing more work and better work than they have done for years, many students do not have a strong picture of schoolwork in their quality worlds. They do very little of what either we or they would call quality work and do not even attend as much as we would like. Nevertheless, as long as they keep school in their quality worlds, we believe that we can persuade them to do more.

But continuation schools are expensive. In business, research shows that it takes five times as much money to find a new customer than to keep a current one satisfied. In school, we start with almost all satisfied customers but spend much less time and effort keeping them satisfied than we do trying to get them back when we have almost lost them. Most students start school with a picture of schoolwork in their quality worlds, and our main effort should be to keep it there. When we do this, we will eliminate the need for expensive alternatives.

School problems do not start immediately. Unless they are so unfortunate as to get a coercive boss-teacher in the first year of school, beginning students are generally eager to do what the teacher asks them to do. They come to school with pictures of school, teachers, and schoolwork, like reading and arithmetic, in their quality worlds because their mothers and others they love have told them that school is good for them and that they will like it. Most kindergarteners and first graders discover that what they have been told is true, and they work hard. Head Start programs have been successful because they increase the strength of the school pictures in many children's quality worlds.

Finding school enjoyable and also wanting to please their parents, young students put the pictures of their caring need-satisfying teachers firmly into their quality worlds. As I have said, the people pictures are most important here. But after the early grades, the number of children who find school satisfying starts to drop significantly. This is because the coercion gets stronger, and students do not feel nearly as good as they did in the lower grades.

For most children, this process accelerates and reaches a peak in the seventh, eighth, or ninth grade, when many students choose to begin removing teachers, schoolwork, and finally school from their quality worlds. Taking this last picture out is not easy, and even those who drop out are rarely willing to remove it completely. Although the picture of school gets very small, most students keep some vestige of it in their quality worlds. They may not like schoolwork or teachers, but they still retain the idea that school itself has value and that they need it.

When asked what is good about school, students all over the country tell me that, good or bad, it is where their friends are. In saying this, they are also telling me that, if the teachers were friendly, few of them would leave school. But when their teachers are coercive where schoolwork is concerned, as has been the experience of most of those who have taken the picture of schoolwork out of their quality worlds, students say that teachers do not care. The students then stop working or leave school altogether. Unless we can get rid of coercion, we will not make even a dent in the problems of education. Anything that smacks of coercion will not be admitted to anyone's quality world.

Many teachers get involved in the same process. Will Rogers is famous for saying, "I never met a man I didn't like," but most teachers have met plenty of students that they don't like. Just as students take teachers out of their quality worlds, teachers take nonworking students out of theirs. As, increasingly, neither sees the other as need-satisfying, the vicious cycle that we see in almost all of our schools begins. This cycle of increasing dislike, distrust, and hostility leads to the adversarial relationship between students and teachers that is so destructive to the purpose of school.

Teaching is a very hard job even when many students are trying, but getting "divorced" students to start working again—a difficult task that many secondary teachers face in almost all their classes—is what makes teaching the hardest of all jobs. We need to learn to become noncoercive lead-managers so that students will find school satisfying enough to keep a picture of it in their quality worlds. The focus must be on prevention. No matter how hard we try to "remotivate" nonworking students who have removed the school picture, I do not think we will ever have much success.

CHAPTER SIX

How We Behave: Quality Work Feels Good

Most successful managers have the luxury of discharging nonproductive workers and looking for better replacements. School managers do not have this option. Poor students cannot be discharged or replaced; large numbers of these students, who produce almost nothing of value, remain in school. To be successful, a school manager has to manage so that almost all the students behave in a way that produces quality work through graduation. To reach this goal, teachers and administrators must learn much more than most of them do now about how we actually behave.

My explanation of choice theory has so far covered why we behave, our needs, and the pictures in our quality worlds. In this chapter I will explain how we behave, a subject much more complicated than most of us realize. First, it is important to accept that all we do from birth to death is behave and that, for all practical purposes, all of our behavior is chosen. We choose to do what we believe will best control the world around us so that it becomes closer to one or more of the pictures we select from our quality world. Our biggest problems arise when we try to control other people. In that sense, we are all trying to be managers, and when we fail it is usually because we depend too much upon the coercive methods of the boss-manager.

Most of us do not realize that no matter how much coercion we use, we cannot consistently control other people: In fact, it is an axiom of choice theory that the only person any of us can consistently control is ourselves. When others do as we ask, it is because they find it more satisfying than anything else they can do at the time. Even when we threaten them, we cannot be sure they will obey, as the holdup example in Chapter Four illustrated. Instead of accepting this axiom and concentrating on managing so that workers can satisfy their needs while doing what we ask, we try again and again to make others do as we want, regardless of how satisfying it may or may not be for them.

For example, if my need for power is satisfied by my son's doing well in school, I may continually badger him to do his homework. But if he refuses, there is nothing I can do to make him do it: All I can actually control is the way I choose to ask him. I can threaten, bribe, sweet-talk, punish, reward, promise the moon, all in the hope that one of these will be persuasive, but I can never be sure that any of these will be. If my son does his homework, it will be because he decided that this was the most satisfying thing that he could do at the time.

Among the most destructive of all our coercive practices is our overuse of personal criticism. We spend too much time telling people we manage that what they are doing is wrong, that they should have done something else in the past instead of what they did, and that their plans for the future are faulty. When we criticize, we often have the advantage of second-guessing, which makes our position safe but increases the anger of those criticized.

More than anything else, if we are to manage successfully, we must do all we can to get in and stay in the quality world of those we manage. The problem with criticism is that it persuades the people we criticize to take us out of their quality world. They see our criticism, constructive as we may think it is, as an attack. It is not constructive to them.

As stated, we cannot consistently control other people; we can control only ourselves. Therefore, the basis of effective lead-managing is to deal with others knowing that you cannot control them, that all you can do is to give them the kind of information that has a good chance of persuading them that the work you ask them to do will feel good as they do it. In practice, workers do not work to satisfy their needs; most do not even know what their needs are. What they want is what we all want—to feel good. If we can help them to feel good, they will listen very carefully to what we ask them to do and, most of the time, will do it.

As we manage workers, especially students, we need to be aware that there are two important aspects of feeling good: immediate and delayed. We all like to feel good all the time, but, as we grow, most of us learn the lesson of the little red hen. We find out that it often pays to endure some immediate short-term pain in order to have a good chance for some later long-term pleasure. Keeping this in mind, what actually leads a worker or a student or anyone to initiate a new behavior is:

1. The behavior the student or worker is presently choosing does not feel very good.
2. The student or worker believes there is something different to do that, sooner or later, will feel better than what he or she is doing now.

The key here is the phrase "sooner or later." Students almost always know what will feel better immediately. If they are bored, they know it will feel good in the short run just to get up and walk out of class. But an effective manager will persuade them that, although an effective behavioral change may not feel good in the short run, there is a very good chance it will feel good in the long run. The little red hen did not enjoy much of the work involved in getting the bread into the oven but she had her eye on the future and it paid off for her.

Whether what the student does feels good immediately or later, what actually initiates all behavioral change is the pain associated with the difference between what the student wants from his or her quality world and what is going on in the real world. The greater or more sudden this difference, the more urgent and energetic the change in behavior will be. A student who is bored may accept the boredom because he or she does not see anything else to do that would be that much better. But a student who is put down by a teacher or a classmate may explode with anger.

In the process of living, most of us have to learn over and over that what feels good in the short run may soon dissipate, that an effective life depends much more on what feels good in the long run than in the short run. In school, much of what students are asked to do does not feel good right away. Because of this, a lead-teacher always tries to manage in a way that the students put the teacher into their quality worlds as a need-satisfying picture. To get into the students' quality worlds, the teacher must have a track record of asking the students to do what feels good in the long run and of asking them to do it in a way that feels good right away. This means that lead-teachers add kindness, courtesy, and humor to whatever they ask students to do.

But besides the immediate caring that gets the job started, the lead-manager will not be effective by only promising long-term satisfaction. Slowly and carefully the manager must help the worker, at the beginning of the job, to gain at least a little short-term satisfaction by providing what the worker appraises is a good place to work. From this, and from caring, the lead-manager can eventually build up to the point that the worker is willing to wait for the long-term satisfaction involved in doing a quality job. Once the workers gain the confidence in the manager's ability to provide the leadership necessary for their long-term satisfaction, they become more and more willing to put up with short-term pain and frustration. It is from this confidence that students become willing to accept the delay in satisfaction that is so much a part of education.

For example, suppose the manager says politely, "I would appreciate it very much if you would sweep the floor, and I have this new electric broom on trial loan. Tell me if it's worth buying." In this way, the manager acknowledges that sweeping is not the best job while involving the worker in the decision to make it better. Few workers would refuse to sweep under these conditions. I am exaggerating to make the point that by consulting the workers, good managers constantly keep the workers' need for power in mind.

Choice theory explains another aspect of our behavior that is critical for managers to understand. As stated earlier, it is important to accept that we choose all of our conscious behavior. If a student does not work in school, that student is choosing not to work. When a teacher attempts to deal with that student, the teacher is also choosing what he or she does.

For example, when students disrupt and refuse to quiet down, many teachers get very upset. But without understanding the choice theory explanation of behavior, an upset teacher will not realize that the upset is how he or she is choosing to deal with frustration. By recognizing that it is a choice, the teacher will learn to choose far better behaviors than to upset. This aspect of choice theory is difficult to understand because when we are upset, we do not feel that we are choosing our misery. Although few people have heard about this concept, it could be very valuable because the idea of making a better choice, instead of continuing to suffer, quickly becomes a very attractive idea to most people.

To clarify why most of us choose so much upset, choice theory explains that behavior is far more than a simple action or activity like moving our legs and arms when we drive a car. It is actually a combination of four separate behavioral components: actions, thoughts, feelings, and physiology. When we look at what we are doing, it is often difficult to appreciate not only that our feelings and physiology are always a part of every behavior, but also that these components are always linked with our actions and thoughts into a whole, or what is best called a total, behavior.

Without choice theory, we tend to look at behavior as made up of a single component—action—or two components—action and thinking. But behavior is never limited to these two components. Can you conceive of a time when you were just thinking and engaging in no action or having no accompanying feelings or being totally devoid of physiology? Except in a deep coma, can your body function without concurrent thoughts? Even when you are asleep, don't you dream as well as move and feel?

Therefore, by saying that we choose all of our behavior, I mean that all behavior is always some blend of acting, thinking, feeling, and physiology. Although we can actually choose two of the four parts of any total behavior, we cannot keep these parts (acting and thinking) separate from the total. Total is total. No matter which part or parts I choose, the other parts are always present.

For example, I can choose to take a walk and also choose, in the beginning, to try to think of nothing but the exercise I will get as I walk. I focus consciously on the action component while I am walking, and I tend not to think much about the other three components: thinking, feeling, and physiology. But I cannot walk unless I initially choose to think, "Start walking," and continue to think, "Keep on walking." After a while, I usually choose other thoughts, and if I get very relaxed, thoughts may intrude from unconscious sources that I do not choose. In almost all cases, I can choose to ignore these extraneous thoughts or certainly choose not to act on them, but I cannot walk (or do anything else) without thinking.

Can I also choose to feel good when I walk? The best I can do when I start out is to think, "I hope I feel good while I walk." But I cannot choose to feel good in the same direct way that I can choose the activity of walking and also choose most of the thoughts that go through my mind as I walk. If I want to feel good while I walk, I must choose to walk at a time and a place, and perhaps with a person, that I know from experience are need-satisfying. If I force myself to get out of a warm bed on a cold, rainy morning, it is very unlikely that I will enjoy the walk.

I cannot choose an action such a taking a walk and feel good if it does not satisfy a need. This is impossible. Both our feelings and physiology work automatically and are proportional to how much or little the thoughts and actions we choose are need-satisfying. For all practical purposes, we cannot feel good or be healthy if we are not mostly choosing thoughts and actions that lead to need-satisfying total behaviors.

For example, suppose someone asks how you are feeling as you are walking. You say, "I feel fine." Then the person asks, "Are you choosing to feel fine?" Here, if you are honest, you might reply, "No, I'm choosing to walk. But since I almost always feel good when I walk, I guess the best I can say is that I'm choosing to do something that usually feels good, and it feels good today."

Suppose the questioner persists by asking, "Suppose you stopped walking right now, could you still feel good?" You would have to say, "I don't know. It all depends on what I'd be doing instead." What you are saying is that you cannot separate what you are doing (actions and thoughts) from your feelings or your physiology. You try to do things that feel good and are healthy, but you do not have nearly as much direct control of how you feel or of your physiology as you do of your actions and thoughts. Sometimes, for reasons you cannot control—like getting bitten by a dog as you walk—the walk turns out miserable.

When students do not work, most teachers are frustrated because they have a picture in their quality worlds of students working hard. Because they are frustrated, they try to choose a managerial behavior that will persuade the students to start working hard. But in this situation, most teachers do not know what to do. Many of them choose to threaten, a coercive choice that often increases the problem and their frustration. But if this is a choice, they also have a choice to ask themselves, "What might be the best way to solve this problem without coercion?" As soon as they think this, they open their minds to better ways to solve the problem because we have almost complete control over our thinking.

Suppose a teacher tells the class that she is disappointed that so few of them are working and that she would like to hear suggestions from them during a class discussion about what could be done to persuade more of them to work. She might say to them, "I am tired of yelling at you. Help me to solve this problem." Suppose the class is doing spelling, and students suggest that the teacher divide the class into four teams and hold a contest to see which team can spell the most words. The idea works, and the students begin to work hard.

How will the teacher feel? How will the class feel? Is the total behavior of discussing a problem better than yelling? Again the answers are obvious. We frequently choose behaviors like yelling and threatening, which do not work and which necessarily feel miserable, but we do not have to choose these behaviors. Once we catch on to the concept of total behavior and understand we always have direct control over our actions and thoughts, we tend to choose actions and thoughts that lead to new and more effective total behaviors that will always have as their feeling components good feelings. But to get these good feelings, we have to choose to act and think in more need-satisfying ways than those that did not get us what we want.

It is interesting that while almost none of us has been able to learn how to choose to feel good directly, almost all of us can make a direct choice to feel bad, to suffer misery, pain, and even sickness. We seem to be able to do this to some extent almost from birth, and we learn a wide variety of additional ways to do this all of our lives. When we are severely frustrated, choosing misery is a very common way of trying to relieve the frustration.

At birth and throughout our lives, we can deal with frustration by choosing anger. We are actually born with the capacity to choose anger; even a very little baby can express a great deal of anger. But anger is only the feeling part of an almost infinite variety of total behaviors of which anger, or angry feelings, may be the most recognizable behavioral component.

From now on, I will call this total behavior *angering* because it makes sense to me to use a verb, not an adjective, to describe behavior. For example, a person may be

old or tall, both adjectives, neither of which has anything
to do with his or her behavior. But if the person is angry,
this is the feeling part of the total behavior he or she is
choosing. As it is also a total behavior, I use the verb forms
angering or choosing *to anger* because the feeling is the
most obvious or recognizable part of this total behavior.

For the most part, the choice to anger is not an effective
way to persuade others to give us what we want. It works
well when we are very small: An angering baby can usually
succeed in getting his parents to jump around as they try to
relieve his frustration. But as we grow older, parents and
others are less and less intimidated by the information that
we are angering. This would usually include coercive
actions and thoughts like yelling and threatening and a
pounding heart, dry mouth, dilated eyes, and tense mus-
cles, which are the physiology of angering.

We begin to learn early to substitute a wide variety of
misery and sickness for the angering because we have
found that the people we need are better controlled
through their "compassioning" when we give them the
information that we are "miserabling" (to keep it all in verb
form). Parents, for example, are much more effectively
controlled by a child who chooses to depress or to sick
than by a child who tantrums. The choice to sick or to miserable can be learned: There are plenty of role models
around. But the child may also figure this out indepen-
dently, as we are capable of figuring out new behaviors,
even miserable ones, when we are frustrated.

In industry and school, managers sometimes have to
deal with people who anger, but more often they have to
deal with people who are depressing, hurting, or sicking as
their way of handling frustration on or off the job. By realizing that this is a choice, the manager is much better able
to deal with these puzzling behaviors successfully. For
example, teachers are aware that young girls of elementary

school age often complain of a stomachache before an important test. In choice theory terms, what they are doing is stomachaching. They create the upset stomach to avoid taking the test because they see themselves as good students and fear a low grade on the test. Stomachaching is their way of getting out of the test.

Teachers who understand choice theory would be able to deal with this effectively. They would know that stomachaching was a choice, and they would concentrate on helping the young students to make better choices. Simply telling them that no single grade is that important and that they will have another chance if they do not do well will usually "cure" the stomachaching. And, of course, if the students do not do well, they must be given the second chance. A lead-manager is never deceptive.

Again, the choice to sick or to hurt is the students' way of dealing with the threat of failure, which is the coercive core of boss-teaching. It is the students' attempt to defend themselves against a need-frustrating coercive system. If it works, as it often does, students learn a self-destructive way to deal with frustration that may last all their lives.

There are certain total behaviors, like drinking, that people choose frequently because they can count on feeling very good when they choose them. What we commonly call vices—drugs, some sexual activity, gambling, overeating— are all total behaviors that people choose when they want to make sure they feel good at least for the short term. But again, the good feeling is not achieved directly: It is still the result of an action that is chosen. And it is not a sure thing. I can eat and/or drink too much and get sick, I can be refused sexually, and I can lose steadily at gambling and not enjoy it at all.

When we have few long-term satisfactions, we are especially attracted to actions that feel good for a while and over which we have a great deal of personal control. This is why there are so many alcohol and drug abusers: Getting high is something we can do easily and immediately all by ourselves. That we are in total control and do not need anyone else is the cornerstone of addiction.

To understand why self-destructive total behaviors like addictions feel good, we must understand that there is a normal physiology of good feelings that is part of every need-satisfying total behavior. Suppose you buy a lottery ticket and then win a big prize. The moment you hear that you have won, you feel ecstatic. Any quick and massively need-satisfying behavior like winning a lottery feels very good because natural pleasure chemicals like endorphins are poured into their brain receptors as the normal physiologic component of this behavior.

What addicting drugs do is to mimic these same chemicals and fill the same receptors in the brain. As they do, they give you the feeling that you have suddenly and massively satisfied your needs. Once you experience this easy, chemically induced pleasure, it becomes hard to forget. The desire to experience it again and again is what leads so many people to pursue an addiction.

One of the most difficult of all management problems is the use of addicting drugs in the workplace by both workers and managers. There are obviously no easy solutions to this problem but the answer lies in increasing the lead-manager approach to managing at all levels. The more work is managed in a way that the workers can obtain long-term satisfaction of their needs through doing quality work, the less they will be attracted to drugs. The more students feel both bored and bossed in school, the more they will be attracted to the easy, immediate pleasure of drugs.

The most sensible school approach to preventing drug abuse is prevention through need-satisfying instruction when the student is young and has not tried drugs. Once dissatisfied students experience the easily attainable good feelings associated with drugs, the less they will be willing to do the work that is necessary for the long-term satisfaction of their needs in school. Students are well aware of the dangers of drugs, but they may ignore them if they are unable to feel good through success in school.

Lead-teachers do not coerce: They talk to their students and work out ways to solve problems. Their students have no need to choose self-destructive total behaviors like acting out, depressing, and drug use. All of these are students' weapons in the adversarial struggle that is characteristic of a boss-managed school. Unlike boss-teachers, lead-teachers do not get angry when they are frustrated because they do not attempt to coerce students into doing what they do not want to do.

Boss-teachers and administrators who grow frustrated and find that angering does not "motivate" many students also choose to suffer a lot. Depressing, headaching, backaching, stomachaching, sicking, and drinking are commonly chosen by frustrated managers, including educators. In many cases, if they did not choose to suffer, they would be too angry to do their job. In some cases, their suffering controls some students, but students are usually the last group to feel compassion for the pain of a frustrated teacher.

What we learn at an early age and never forget is that people who care for us personally or legally can be controlled by our paining or sicking. We also learn that we can control ourselves through choosing paining or sicking. We learn for example, to substitute depressing for angering because it is a much safer thing to do. If we anger, we may do something destructive like hurt someone and even spend time in jail. When we choose to depress, we do not usually have the energy to destroy anything or hurt anyone so that depressing is one of the safest ways to deal with a frustration we cannot seem to solve. Most of us learn to depress early in life, and later we learn similar miserable behaviors like headaching and worrying, which serve the same purpose for many of us. Exactly how we do this is too complicated to explain in this book, but that we do it in many cases is obvious.[1]

Caring for employees who pain and sick is now a very large part of the modern workplace. The newspapers carry many ads soliciting people to make a claim against an employer for "causing stress" on the job. It may be that some employers treat workers so badly that they have no other choice but to choose to suffer, but this is rare. More likely, workers do not like the job because they see themselves as insignificant or powerless at work, a situation in which many boss-teachers, who teach in difficult schools, find themselves. Then they learn to choose a total behavior that includes suffering or sicking so that they can receive compensation from a "compassionate" workers' compensation system.

After they have been compensated, usually not adequately in their opinion, they usually make some sort of a recovery, but not always. Sometimes, through the suffering, they get what they consider to be enough control over their lives so that they never choose to recover. The unfortunate result of this growing failure to deal more effectively with paining or sicking is that huge sums of money are paid to doctors, lawyers, and others who make a living helping these people. All of this huge expense and waste of talent is created by a boss-managed system that is coercive and frustrating. What we need is more lead-management so that this money could be paid to employees for quality work instead of draining most of it away from the workers as we do now. Unfortunately, suffering or disability, for those who choose it, has a huge payoff; its only serious flaw is that it is miserably uncomfortable. This is the price, however, that millions of people, old and young, are willing to pay.

Suffering teachers, also, are hardly the best people to handle frustrated students. And as long as students are frustrated, teachers will be frustrated too. There is no way a manager can be happy if the workers do not produce. Teachers need to learn that only by choosing to teach in a need-satisfying way can they satisfy both their own needs and the needs of their students.

Managers, including teachers, who want to be successful have to learn to counsel workers who choose angering, depressing, or some other miserabling that seems to be getting in the way of their doing quality work. Counseling is talking to workers or students with the purpose of helping them to choose more need-satisfying total behaviors as they work.

For example, a teacher may find it almost impossible to teach grammar to an angry, often truant student who tells the teacher that she hates school and does not want to be in the teacher's class. Is there any doubt that the student is choosing not to try to learn? While she may not be aware of the fact that she is also choosing her anger, from her standpoint, as long as the teacher pressures her to learn what she does not want to learn, has she any other choice but to mobilize the angering that she frequently chooses when she is frustrated? If she does not show her anger, wouldn't she be acting and still be angry underneath? Can she stop her heart from pounding or her hands from sweating if she is confronted with her flaws? No. These are the natural emotions and physiology that go along with the rebellious actions and thoughts that led to the confrontation.

But, as I will explain in greater detail in Chapter Ten when I discuss counseling nonproductive students, it does no good for the manager to focus on the students' feelings or physiology. This is because we cannot directly change either of these components. The manager needs to be sensitive and compassionate to the students' upsets, yet focus as much as possible on the behavioral components the students can change—their actions and thoughts. Unless the student previously mentioned changes her actions and thoughts so that she does better in her English class, there is little likelihood that she will stop feeling angry or upset in that class.

Counseling an upset worker whose work is not satisfactory becomes one of the tests of managing that lead-managers have a good chance to pass and boss-managers almost always fail. This is why many managers, especially teachers, are so puzzled. They see themselves as noncoercive human beings who are caring and sensitive, and they make an effort to talk to their students or workers warmly and noncoercively where work is not directly concerned. But when they go back to managing "in order to get the work done," they become coercive and send a mixed message to the workers. The coercive side of this mixed message almost always erases the counseling side. The workers, sensing the coercion much more than the noncoercion, do not buckle down and do the quality work, which is the only way to solve the problem.

Therefore, as important as it is to be compassionate to the workers' feelings and health, if the manager does not focus on helping the workers without coercion to act and think more effectively on the job, the manager will not be successful. I will explain in detail how to do this in Chapters Nine and Ten, when I discuss how to handle students who do not follow the rules.

Although our modern, media-dominated society sends the message that we should all be happy all the time, there is nothing wrong with being frustrated. No one can live in Shangri-la. When we are frustrated, we must try to act and think more effectively, and in so doing find a total behavior that will reduce or end the frustration. What we can do, and only we can do it (a machine cannot), is create a new behavior. Everything that exists in the world that is the result of human effort was created by someone who was frustrated with the status quo. Even the expressions on our faces or the timbre of our voices is constantly being created as we to try to communicate what we want to express in the best possible way.

If we were more aware of this process and more open to the creative ideas that are continually bubbling up inside us, we would be better able to deal with frustration. A manager who encourages the expression of creativity in workers will find that this unique ability can solve many problems that are resistant to the prosaic solution of just working harder.

When we put all this information together—the needs, the pictures in our quality world, our total behavior, and our ability to create completely new behaviors—we have the basics of choice theory. As we have seen, it is called choice theory because it states that we are always trying to choose behavior in a way that best satisfies our needs. And as we do, we must realize that we should not waste time and effort trying to control other people. It is not until we become knowledgeable and accepting of choice theory that we finally realize that all we can control is our own behavior: We cannot directly control anyone else.

The more a manager focuses on the needs that are hardest to satisfy—belonging and power—and figures out how to manage in such a way that these needs are satisfied, the more successful he or she will be. Managers who manage in a way that empowers workers are by far the most successful because it is harder for most of us to satisfy our need for power than any of our other needs. This is especially true in school: Students who feel powerless make up the vast majority of those who do not work in school.

Choice theory is not abstract. It is usable every day of our lives and is especially useful for managers. Although teaching effectively is the hardest of all managerial jobs, it can be made easier if teachers are willing to try to incorporate choice theory into the way they approach the job.

CHAPTER SEVEN

Quality Schoolwork

Anyone who understands choice theory would predict what Deming has found to be true: Workers will not work hard unless they believe there is quality in what they are asked to do. Working hard will not satisfy our need for power when we are engaged in doing what we believe is a low-quality task: Busy work, for example, is the epitome of low-quality schoolwork. Although quality may be a hard concept to define, most of us recognize it when we see it, and most students do not see it in the work they are asked to do in their academic classes. On the other hand, they easily see the quality inherent in most of their extracurricular activities. They recognize quality music and drama, and they know a good football team when they see one.

When they volunteer for extracurricular activities, students work hard because they want the fun, freedom, power, and sociability that are associated with these activities and that are actually what gives them quality. In fact, because these activities are voluntary, they become more attractive; freedom of choice adds quality to what we choose. If all students were expected to play football, there would obviously be much less quality to this activity. But whether our activities are voluntary or not, when we fail to recognize that there is quality in what we do, we will not work hard to do it.

For example, on any given day in an average nonvoluntary academic class like tenth-grade English, fewer than ten students will be working hard. The rest will be doing little more than sitting there.[1] If you ask the nonworking students why they are not working, they will say that the class is boring, that they don't need it, or that no one cares what they think. While the work may have value to the teacher, the students do not see much value in what they are being asked to do.

If you ask the slackers why the few students who are working are making the effort, they will make a few disparaging remarks about the type of students who work (*nerds* is the current word), but it will be apparent that they really don't know the answer. Then ask those who are working why they are doing so. They will say that they need a good grade or that they don't want to disappoint their parents much more often than they will say that the work has value or quality. More than almost any workplace, school, with its many compulsory academic subjects, suffers from its inability to project an image of quality to the work the workers are asked to do.

When students say that they hate school, much of what they are saying is they hate being asked to work hard at something that does not fulfill their needs. Many of these same students will say that what they want is to get out of school and go to work. Right now there are unskilled and semiskilled part-time jobs available, and many young people are working much harder at after-school jobs at fast-food restaurants than they do in school. This is because most of them see what they are asked to do at work, menial as it is, as more need-satisfying than schoolwork. While the money is satisfying, there is another factor operating that is more subtle. For most of them, it is easier to see the quality in what they are asked to do at work—for example, be clean, courteous, and quick—than to see the quality of the reading and calculating they do at school. I don't believe this would continue if these students felt that they had to work the rest of their lives at a fast-food restaurant, but in the short run what is high quality at McDonald's is more obvious to them than what is high quality in English or math.

On the other hand, and this may seem contradictory, if you ask students working at McDonald's if they want a good education, the answer will be Yes. They have a vague picture in their quality worlds of what they conceive to be a good education, but I believe few of them have any idea of what it actually is. It is easier for them to see quality on the job than at school. To find out why requires a few more questions.

If you ask if it takes hard work to get a good education, students will again answer Yes. They are still not clear about what a good education is, but whatever it may be, they think it takes hard work to get it. Further, if you ask them if they are smart enough to get a good education, almost all will answer Yes, even if they do not know exactly what it is they have to be smart enough to do.

But if you then ask them if they are working hard in school, most will answer No. What they are saying is that, as much as they want the vague something that to them is a good education and know it takes hard work to get it, they do not have any clear idea of how schoolwork, as they now know it, relates to what they want. Until they have a much clearer idea about what a quality education is and how it can be attained from what they are asked to do, students will not work hard in school.

This is hardly a problem exclusive to schools. It is a problem inherent in any work situation where there is little emphasis on achieving quality. For example, the American auto industry produced low-quality cars for years and years, and no one seemed to care. In the same vague sense that students want a "good" education, both the auto workers and those who managed them wanted to build a "quality" car: Unfortunately, however, they did not know what a good car was any more than most students have a clear, tangible idea of what a good education is. But once cars made in Japan, Germany, and Sweden began to come into this country, it became obvious what a quality car was.

As soon as customers woke up to the fact that there was a car with more quality than they had thought possible, many of them stopped buying American cars even when the imports became more expensive. Even many American auto workers started buying foreign-built cars. Suddenly people knew what a good car was, and they wanted one.

Now American automakers have finally become aware that to survive they must build a better car, and Deming certainly helped them. To do it, however, they have had to change to the beginnings of lead-management; the traditional boss-managers could not coerce the workers into making the effort to build a better car in quantity. Many American cars are much better because of this management change. The workers now recognize that there is more satisfaction and more job security in building a better product, and they seem to be willing to work harder and more carefully than they did before. Unfortunately, it will not be as easy to find a recognizable quality education model as it was to find a high-quality car, but once quality is recognized as the answer to the problems, we will at least begin to look for these models—an important first step.

As mentioned in earlier chapters (and documented by Linda McNeil), the problem is that even the possibility of finding quality in education has been made much more difficult by the increasing boss insistence that all academic subjects be fragmented into small "objective" bits to be measured on achievement tests. Some students work hard to master this low-quality material because they see it as necessary for college, which is very much a picture in their quality worlds. Most, however, see no quality in the type of study needed to do well on these tests, and students who do not have a firm picture of college in their quality worlds will not study very hard for them. This is a major reason why scores are slipping: Fewer and fewer students are willing to do this much work when there is nothing in the work itself that has much value to them.

As Linda McNeil pointed out, we are making the serious mistake of assuming that a high-quality school is one where students are orderly and get low-quality "passing" scores on non-quality achievement tests. Led (really misled) by state departments of education, we are striving to do in our schools what, had it continued, would have destroyed the auto industry. Ill-designed, poorly-built cars were able to pass minimal inspection standards; not knowing better or having no better ones available, people bought them. People are still supporting our schools, but their discontent is increasing. If better models were more widely available and publicized, people would demand the same from their school systems.

Huntington Woods Elementary in Wyoming, Michigan, is probably, as of this writing in 1998, one of the best models in the United States of what could be called a quality school. Even at Huntington Woods, however, the staff would be the first to admit that there is still work to be done before *all* students put schoolwork into their quality worlds. But we need more than a few models. No one paid attention to the quality foreign cars until they arrived in quantity.

When I talk to students, as I do frequently, I have begun to ask them questions about quality. There is no doubt that they know both what quality is and that to achieve it takes a great deal of hard work. When I ask them whether they have done much quality work in school, at first many say that they have. But when I ask them how many times they have actually worked hard enough to do the best work they possibly could, almost none, including the very good students, say that they have ever done as much as they are capable of doing. I think it is safe to say that very few students expend the effort to do quality work in school.

But I think it is also safe to say that those who manage our schools do not manage for quality and that most teachers do not even think of quality when they address the students in their classes. On their minds are the goals of those who manage at the top of the system: raising the test scores; getting more students through; keeping discipline problems low. There is no way that anyone will ever confuse these minimal goals with quality. The result is that less than 15 percent of all students do quality work. When quality suddenly appears in classes where it had never been before, as in the movie *Stand and Deliver,* it is so unusual that it borders on the unbelievable and becomes the stuff of real-life drama.

When we do quality work, we carefully evaluate what we are doing and come to the conclusion that it is worth working hard to continue to do it because it feels good. What few managers realize is that the coercion boss-managers use prevents this necessary self-evaluation because the workers or students spend most of their time and effort evaluating the boss instead of evaluating their own work.

For an illustration of this point, consider the example in Chapter One of the students at West High in Torrance who purposely failed the state assessment tests because they resented the amount of time that preparation for these low-quality tests took from the high-quality work that they felt they should be doing. The students focused their

resentment on the boss-administrators they saw as pushing this meaningless assessment program. They then did
what we all tend to do when we are being coerced: wasted
time and effort evaluating the coercers and trying to out-
wit them. If they had not been coerced, these students
would have ignored the tests and spent this same time
and effort furthering their education by evaluating their
own work and raising its quality. And they still would
have done reasonably well on the tests they made so
much effort to mess up. When effort is diverted from the
task to be done, as happens in every coercive situation,
quality must suffer.

Let me give another example to illustrate this difficult
point. Suppose you are involved in a minor car accident
and you recognize that it was partly your fault. But the
other driver comes on very strong and blames you for the
whole thing. Immediately you forget about the part that
was your fault and defend yourself by trying to place all the
blame on the other driver. The same thing happens in
school. Even though most of what students are asked to do
in school has the potential for quality, students so resent
being coerced that they spend their time hating school
instead of evaluating their work and trying to improve it.

When we are coerced, we usually refuse to take owner-
ship of the work we are asked to do. But for students to do
quality work, it is crucial that they see that it is for their
benefit, not the benefit of their teachers, school system, or
parents. Think of the times in your life when you did high-
quality work. Didn't you do it because you were supported
and encouraged enough so that you were willing to evaluate what you were doing and work to get better and better?
As you improved, didn't the work itself became more and
more important to you? Or did you do it because you were
badgered and wanted to get rid of the pressure from the
manager or teacher?

In education more than industry, it is the rare student who can recognize quality when he or she starts a new subject. In the movie *Stand and Deliver*, the true story of a group of Hispanic-American high school students who successfully learned calculus, it is clear that the students did not have any idea that there was quality to calculus when they started. What they recognized quickly, however, was that their teacher, Jaime Escalante, was a high-quality teacher, and they began to accept that if he taught calculus, it, too, must have quality.

These students first put Escalante's picture into their quality worlds, and when they began to succeed at learning this difficult subject—a feat few had ever dreamed they could do—they added calculus to this same world. Finding this effort need-satisfying, they began to work harder than they had ever worked in school. I am sure many teachers have had a similar experience: First they were accepted as quality instructors; then their students got successfully involved in what was taught and began to experience the pleasure of achieving quality. It was this pleasure that led students to continue to do the hard work that led them to the top rung of scholastic success.

As stated earlier, to be accepted into students' quality worlds the teacher has to become a lead-manager: Those you manage must sense your concern that the work you ask them to do be done in a way that satisfies their needs, especially their need for power. Even if, in the beginning, there is not much need-satisfaction possible in the work you ask them to do, your concern that there be some need-satisfaction helps persuade students to see you as a quality teacher. In a quality school system, you will also be seen as part of a whole system that is concerned that all students get involved in quality education.

Quality is not the image that most school systems project because they make the serious mistake of accepting what is obviously low-quality schoolwork starting in the very early grades. A student in any grade from first to twelfth may turn in what is to him, and to anyone else, a minimal assignment or test and hope that this is the end of that task. Most of the time this is the case: We accept what the student turns in, whether or not we believe that he could do better. We deal with the low quality by giving the student a low grade. This is the end of both his and our work on that paper or test.

A quality school would not accept low-quality work from any student. (Refer to the description in Chapters Three and Four of how a lead-teacher would teach algebra.) Beginning in the first grade and continuing through school, the subject of quality and how it relates to school-work would be discussed with students so that they have a clear idea that quality work, at least as the teachers and administrators see it, is the goal of the school. Examples of quality work would be posted, and students would be encouraged to judge what they do for quality.

As stated in the first chapter, this is not hard to do. Most students and teachers would agree that the work exhibited in their school is high quality. In actuality, the problem is to judge what quality is not as much as what it is. This process should begin the day school starts and continue to the end of the year.

Once students have an awareness of quality and are told that quality work is the goal of the school, they should be asked if they would accept this goal. They would immediately ask if hard work was involved, and they should be told that it is: There is no way to achieve quality without hard work. In *Stand and Deliver*, Escalante made no secret of the amount of work that would be involved, but since the work began to be need-satisfying, most students were willing to do it. Students should also be told that they, as much as their teachers, will be the judge of the quality of what they do. Then it should be explained both to them and to their parents why raising the state test scores a point or two or reducing the dropout rate a few percentage points are no longer the goals of this school: The new goal is quality in all that takes place in school.

While the teacher must be the final judge of the quality of the work students do, I suggest that, starting in the first grade, students be asked to evaluate all their work in writing and sign it before turning it in. I have talked to high school students about quality work, and most of them would be willing to do this ongoing evaluation. If it were started early in a lead-managed elementary school, I think almost all students would accept this procedure. Some high school students, however, many of whom admitted that they had never done any quality schoolwork, said that they would not do this evaluation of their work. When I asked them why, they told me that this was not their job, it was the teacher's, another example of boss-managed students focusing on the teacher instead of on the material to be learned. When pushed as to why it was not their job to evaluate their own work, they told me that if they began to assess their work honestly, they would have to work much harder.

Choice theory explains that what these students were really saying was that if they willingly took a good look at what they usually do in school, their need for power would make it very hard for them to write "low quality" on an assignment and sign it. As long as they do not do this, it is easy to blame the teacher, especially if the teacher is coercive, for boring assignments or low grades and to avoid taking responsibility for the low-quality work they do. What I think some of the students were also saying was that they do not want to take responsibility for assessing assignments that they do not think have the potential for much quality. Busy work will have to be eliminated; no one wants to assess what is seen as low-quality work. It also goes without saying that this request for assessment will suffer to the extent that students do not see the teacher as a quality person.

Assuming the work has the potential, like calculus, to be seen as high quality, the student should be asked to improve any work that is assessed as low quality. The work should not be accepted until both the student and the teacher agree that it is of substantially better quality. A good grade should be given for the improved work.

To get this process started in a school where it is completely new, it might be reasonable initially to accept work if it has been improved in any obvious way. This is because students who are asked to labor too long on an assignment or test before they have made the shift to quality work will grow tired of it and refuse to extend much effort. By being asked for some improvement, the students will begin to recognize that what is wanted is higher quality work and that even if they did not do it at first, it needs to be done and they can do it. If this is done in a noncoercive, nonadversarial, lead-manager atmosphere, the students will see this as a need-satisfying way to work that they have not experienced before. They will appreciate this way of working and begin to like school much more than when they were boss-managed and accepted as low-quality workers.

While posting and discussing examples of good work will be helpful to students who are trying to learn what quality is, there is no substitute for what students learn when they do a quality job themselves. This is one of the reasons why students work so hard in their extracurricular activities; they know first-hand how good it feels to do something well that is important to them. To an aspiring basketball player, shooting 300 free throws after practice is not busy work. Until students begin to work this hard in class, we will never achieve much quality in our schools.

Exams should be handled slightly differently from class assignments. Tests should be completed by students individually or, if they are working cooperatively, by the student teams. The students should continue to work on the test until all answers are correct or satisfactory. While on other assignments the teacher may settle for some improvement, this should not be the case for tests. The standard should be that no matter how long it takes, all questions must be answered satisfactorily. There should be no such thing as low- or even medium-quality performance on a test: Only high quality should be acceptable.

When the program starts, it may be necessary to give shorter tests, but not necessarily easier ones. No student should proceed to the next test until he or she has correctly completed the last one. Some courses may have to be extended, but anything less than this approach will compromise the move to quality that is the major goal of a lead-managed school.

Since there will be much reworking and improving, especially in the beginning, it would be helpful if the school could develop a core of volunteer tutors to help students both individually and in groups. Tutoring is an obvious solution to many of the problems that will arise. Some schools may decide to put these ideas into place all at once, and others may introduce them one class at a time. My inclination would be to go slowly and introduce them only in classes where both teachers and students accept what has to be done.

But quality goes beyond doing well on tests and assignments. We need to strive for the students setting their own standards for quality, not just doing well according to the teacher. Deming points out that given the encouragement and tools, workers will build better products than boss-managers have ever dreamed possible and will improve them even more as time goes on.

This is obvious when we see the record-breaking performances of athletes in the Olympic games. In many cases, the athletes performed far beyond the expectations of even their coaches. But even if they did not win, what they were proud of was that, as good as they were, they had improved. In other words, the idea of quality had taken hold inside them. This is what we need to try to do with our students: Start very early and talk to them about quality. Give them tools and lots of encouragement. Then stand back and see where they go once the idea of quality education gets inside their heads.

As I write this chapter, I can see people with power, like school board members, saying, "This is a great idea! Let's 'make' students improve the quality of their work." The problem is that we cannot make people do anything well. We have to take the lead-approach and slowly introduce them to quality. If there is any coercion, they will shift the focus from their work to their coercers. To the extent that they do, quality will be lost in the process.

While there is much to be worked out as these ideas are put into practice, Deming has shown that "working it out" is the easiest part. The hardest part is deciding to do it and getting rid of the adversarial, boss-managed atmosphere that is so destructive to all that we are attempting to do. There is no guarantee that we will achieve quality using what has been suggested here, but there is good evidence that if we do not do something like this, we will never achieve it. The good news is that quality is contagious, and we see this contagion in extracurricular activities. Students do not have to be coerced to put effort into playing basketball, singing in the chorus, or participating in the school play.

If we can achieve quality in our classes, as I believe we can, then academic quality will also become contagious. Many students who work hard now are treated like pariahs by the other students because the "accepted" student attitude in our boss-managed, adversarial schools is to be anti-education. The only way to defeat this destructive attitude is to make quality as much a part of our academics as it is now a part of athletics. Once quality becomes a part of our classes, students will be proud of what they do and this pride will become as contagious as pride anywhere. It is obvious that few students or teachers are proud of what goes on now in too many of our classes.

While we may never be able to define quality in school in any exact way, if both teachers and students work steadily to achieve it through noncoercive self-evaluation, they may reach it even without being able to define it. For those who want to learn more about this complex subject, the ideas related to it are beautifully expressed in Robert Pirsig's definitive work on quality, *Zen and the Art of Motorcycle Maintenance.*[2]

My definition of quality is "whatever we put into our quality world," and unless, through lead-management, many more students than now put schoolwork into this world we will not solve many of the problems we face. What I am suggesting is a huge restructuring of basic educational practice based on choice theory and managed by lead-managers. There are, however, many details that must be worked out. In the next chapter, I will take a close look at some of these details.

CHAPTER EIGHT

Grades and Other Basics of a Quality School

"Define a good student." I ask this of small groups of students, usually from junior or senior high school, when I interview them in front of teacher groups. The students answer as anyone else would: works hard; does the best he or she can; has a good attitude; does what the teacher says; does not give the teacher a hard time. Then I ask them to be more specific. "What kind of grades does a good student get?" Even though those selected to be interviewed are almost always good students, they are uncomfortable with this question. They say that grades are not important: What is important is that good students try their best. They usually add, "It's not necessary to get all A's to be a good student." But I keep pushing, "Does a good student get any C's?" And they answer, "Maybe." Then I ask, "Do any of you get C's?" Usually they tell me that they do not, but they continue to insist that C's are acceptable. I ask, "Would your parents accept a C grade?" And they tell me that C's are not welcome in their homes.

The students are trying not to appear conceited because they personally get good grades, but it is obvious, as we carry on the discussion, that good grades are very important both to them and to their parents. From these discussions I also learn that fewer than half the students in their school are good students as they have just defined good students, which means getting A's and B's, no C's. I then ask them, "Do the students who get mostly C's or less ever improve their grades to A's and B's?" The students doubt this ever happens. They tell me that occasionally some C students do well in a class where the teacher conducts discussions or uses cooperative learning, but mostly the C students do not participate in discussions, and if they work at all in cooperative groups, it is to copy from the one or two good students doing the work. If the students were describing a factory, more than half the workers would be receiving minimum wages and doing less than minimal work. Many would even be interfering with the better workers as they tried to work.

I then ask, "Would the poor students like to get good grades?" "Yes," they answer, but add that most of them hate school and won't do the work. When asked why the poor students hate school, they reply that these students do not believe the teachers care about them or what they do. The idea that students who do not work believe that no one in the school cares about them is very strong with all students. When I get an occasional group of poor students to interview, they confirm what the good students have said: They would like to get good grades, but the work is boring and nobody cares, so they don't make the effort.

Finally, I ask both the good and the poor students, "Are the poor students incapable of getting good grades? Are they as a group less capable than the good students?" They assure me that this is rarely the case. They say that if the C and D students worked hard they could do as well as anyone else, and I believe them. We are not talking about inability; we are talking about not working. We are also looking at a situation that both the students and the teachers in a boss-managed school accept: As time goes on, the A and B students will separate from the C, D, and F students, and by high school they will hardly know each other. As choice theory clearly explains, once students get low grades they start to take school out of their quality worlds. They do less work and separate from the students who are working.

Even if we are able to make the move to quality schools, grades, the most sacred of all the educational cows, are here to stay. Good students want grades because they represent good pay for good work. Teachers want them because they do not want to lose the power to use grades to coerce: "Do as I say and you'll get a good grade; don't and you'll get a bad grade." As I will shortly explain, a quality school will retain good grades because, if they are fairly earned, their coercive power is not destructive: It is like higher pay for better work. Little will be lost, however, when bad grades are eliminated. If bad grades have any coercive value at all, it disappears when the high and low groups divide. For students who get them after elementary school, they are like beating a dead horse. By the eighth grade, most students and teachers know after a few weeks of school who is going to get a good grade and who a bad grade.

Through a combination of low test scores, failure to hand in assignments, and cutting class, many students know early in the school year they are going to fail a course. When these students are sent to a counselor for misbehavior or no effort, the counselor can do nothing to "motivate" them. Counseling a student in this dead-end situation is like trying to get a condemned man to plan for the future.

In a quality school, there are no bad grades. My guess is that this will be the single most difficult change to make. Teachers, administrators, parents, and politicians will complain that they are being asked to disarm in the middle of a war. Even some students who get good grades may resist. It will take time, patience, and effort to convince teachers to give up the threat of a bad grade, but unless bad grades, with all their potential for coercion, can be totally removed from a school, it will not become a quality school.

Eliminating bad grades does not have to be done quickly. It can and probably should begin slowly with teachers who understand and accept the idea behind this change. Before teachers eliminate low grades in their classes, they should consult parents, explain the reasons for this change, and obtain their agreement to a trial of this approach. If this new way to grade is effective, other teachers will be willing to try. For obvious reasons, in a quality school no attempt would be made by the administration to coerce any teacher into making this change until he or she was ready.

In any school, grades have two major purposes:

1. To give information to students, their parents, and others who may be interested, like colleges, in how well the student is doing.
2. To serve as a substitute for pay.

High grades are a reward for quality work and are very satisfying to students' need for power. In a quality school, however, permanent low grades would be eliminated. A low grade would be treated as a temporary difficulty, a problem to be solved by the student and the teacher working together, with the hope that the student would come to the conclusion that it is worth expending more effort. But besides low grades, any grade, even an A, could be improved at almost any time if the student can demonstrate to the teacher that he or she is now more productive than before. Grades, like pay, should always be tied to increased productivity.

Where a quality school would differ substantially from a traditional school is that only the courses in which students had done quality work would be recorded on their transcripts. The lowest grade that would indicate quality work would be a B; for even better work, A and A+ would be recorded. It is important that a B be at least as good as it is now: What is now a C should not become a B in a quality school. There is no sense doing what we do now, which is to record, with a low grade, the fact that the student has not mastered the material. For example, if a student's transcript in a quality school lists algebra followed by a B, then anyone reading that record will know that the student is competent in this subject. If the grade is A or A+, the student is more than competent: He is skilled. If, in the unlikely case, the student has struggled with algebra for several years and has still not done quality work, there would be no indication of the course on the student's transcript. In a quality school, the record shows what students know, not what they do not know. The record, however, would not show how long it took to master the subject as that could, in some instances, be coercive.

This means that the coercive or punitive C's, D's, and F's that we use so liberally now would be eliminated completely from the permanent transcript. C would be retained, but it would be restricted to temporary use only. As all students would be asked to evaluate all of their work, students who give themselves C's, or are given C's by the teacher, would be put on notice that they have not done a quality job on that test or assignment. This would become a problem that the teacher would like to help the student solve and that the teacher also believes can be solved. Given the warm, supportive environment of the quality school where there is no failure, and where there is almost always the possibility of tutoring, it would be more need-satisfying for students to work to raise their grades than to give up and receive no credit for the course.

Grading should never be on a curve: No student's grade should ever depend on what other students do. Since the purpose of the school is to produce quality work, many students will get high grades. This is not grade inflation: It is representative of what the students have learned. The reasoning behind the elimination of grades below B is the same as the elimination of minimal pay in a successful business. No business that wants to succeed in the long run can afford the "luxury" of low wages because low-paid workers will not expend the effort necessary to make quality products or perform quality services.

A quality product is not an average product or a minimal product. Would you want to be operated on by an average surgeon or eat an average meal in a restaurant? No one wants anything average, so why should we settle in school for the low quality that is now average? Lead-managers manage for quality because they know that less has little value. They are confident they can achieve it, and they are more than willing to pay good wages to the workers who produce that quality.

The space shuttle *Challenger* was a classic example of a C product produced by boss-management. The top managers did not listen to lower managers, and there is some indication that no one at the top listened to the workers. Because of this, the workers did only enough to get by, and a low-quality product was put into space. This is confirmed by the fact that after the disaster more than 200 improvements, many of them major, were made in the design and fabrication of the shuttle.

Even though C or lower is an acceptable grade in much of our society, it should not be an acceptable grade in school. In fact, I doubt if we will improve our society until we make the effort to move to quality schools. Lead-managers do not manage for C work, and they do not see workers as C people. Therefore, every effort is made to see that there are no long-term C students or permanent C work in a quality school. B work, which means competent work, is the lowest acceptable performance.

But what if students work hard, keeping school in their quality worlds, and still do not produce good work? The answer is that in a quality school this would be almost impossible. Anyone, student or not, who works hard at a job he believes he can do will produce good work if given enough time. If a student tells the teacher that he does not believe he can do the job in the class he is in, he would be counseled to move to a class where he believes he can succeed. There is no more sense in trying to make a student do what he believes he cannot do than trying to make a factory worker lift what he cannot budge.

In Garfield High in Los Angeles, all students do not take calculus. But almost all students who take calculus succeed.[1] In a quality school, courses that require a large amount of talent or aptitude would be open to all. Students who had difficulty, even if they worked hard, would be counseled to try to do what they had more aptitude to do, but this would not be a big problem. This is because neither we nor most students have any clear idea what most students can do because too many do not have schoolwork in their quality worlds. I believe there is very little offered in our schools that students could not do if they put it into their quality worlds.

It would be easy to get this quality grading system operational if it were started in the first grade. It would be harder to start it with older students who do not believe they can do quality work because they have never worked hard and have always received low grades. The key with these students is to persuade them to do one piece of quality work in school, and through this another, and then slowly persuade them to begin to put quality schoolwork into their quality worlds. To do this, however, they have to get at least a B. No one will do quality work without good pay.

To get an A in any subject, students would do what is ordinarily A work now. What would be different in a quality school is the grade A+. This grade should be reserved for any student who does work above the quality that ordinarily is given an A. Teachers in each course would set the criteria for this A+ work, but I suggest that it be given to students who, on their own, do something significant that is beyond what the teacher or the course required. This means that, using their own ingenuity and creativity, the students demonstrate that they have moved beyond the course requirements. For example, students might complete a voluntary science or computer project, apply what has been learned in the community by helping to solve environmental problems, tutor other students to competency—anything that shows the student went well beyond what is ordinarily required for an A.

This grade would be very valuable for college entrance, and it would help to quell the fears of the parents of the 15 percent of students who do well now. Many of these parents want to maintain low grades so that, in contrast to the others, their children can easily be seen to excel. In many instances only the very intelligent or the very gifted will have a chance to receive the A+ grade, but even they will still have to work hard to earn it. This is another way in which the quality school would differ from today's schools, in which gifted students frequently get A's without doing much work. To get the top grade, A+, in a quality school, even those who were lucky in their genetic endowment would have to work hard. Many capable people do little with their lives because they never learned the value of hard work.

STATE AND DISTRICT ASSESSMENT TESTS

The quality school should not concern itself with outside measures of productivity, such as state-mandated achievement tests, because these machine-scored tests do not measure quality. If they have a purpose, it is to pick up the failure of many students to reach the minimal standards of boss-managed schools. The Advanced Placement (AP) calculus test that Escalante's students did so well on is a much better test.[2] Only a portion of this test is machine scored, and it does a fair job of measuring quality learning in this subject.

A quality school would be encouraged to try to involve students in the AP program through which they can earn college credits in high school. The AP tests are so far ahead of the machine-scored assessment tests that there would be little relationship between what goes on in the quality school to prepare students to pass AP exams and what is now done to prepare students for state assessment. Because of this, and also because the state-mandated tests are so far removed from what education is supposed to be, it is possible that lead-managed schools would not do well on them. But they will not do badly either. Basically, there should be no problem with these tests.

For college entrance, the lead-managed school will have special sessions devoted to studying for these noneducational exercises, and students who need good scores on these tests will be encouraged to attend. Students who graduate from a quality school and do well in college would be encouraged to come back and lead the sessions.

To prepare for this tutoring, they might take one or more of the special courses now offered by private companies and add what they have learned from the "experts" to what they teach in these cram courses.

RECORD KEEPING, STATISTICS, AND TEACHER TRAINING

Deming maintains that the only way to improve quality is to keep statistics so that you know whether the organization is going forward, moving backward, or standing still where quality is concerned. In the lead-managed school a careful record should be kept of each student's progress. While I am not an expert on school record keeping, there is no shortage of people who could do this once they've mastered the concepts of a quality school. For example, if we move to quality in algebra and find that it takes two years for most students to achieve at least the B that indicates competency, this amount of time should be allocated. Right now algebra is given a year, and even our flawed testing system shows that most students do not become competent in that time. Those who do not learn are either given low grades or failed, which persuades many of them to take math out of their quality worlds for life. When they do, we lose them for the technical work our society increasingly needs.

The way we run schools now there is no way to learn if more time is needed to achieve quality. Not only do we not try to teach all students to achieve quality, but there is no record of how long it takes to reach it. There is only a record of how many students have reached A, B, C, D, or F in a year. I cannot see how these data can possibly provide the information we need to tell us how long it takes to learn algebra well given the present way it is taught in most schools. If we tell our math teachers that they are doing an inadequate job and fail to give them the time they need to do an adequate job, then how can they possibly improve?

Statistics should also be kept as to which is the best way to teach. This means keeping a record of how long it takes a group of algebra teachers who use different approaches to teach comparable students to the B level of competence or quality. For example, did the teachers who used cooperative learning do better or worse than the teachers who did not use it? Did the teachers who assigned more homework reach the level of quality quicker than the teachers who assigned less? The purpose of doing this is not to point out who is more or less effective but to learn what the more effective teachers do that others could learn to do.

Deming says, "Institute training on the job." But he also points out firmly that training is worthless unless there is some statistical proof that what people are trained to do works. If we suspect that someone is a great teacher, we need to back that suspicion up with statistical proof. The framework of the grading system suggested for the quality school would make getting this proof much easier than now. From the standpoint of quality, almost all of the money now spent on state and local assessment tests is wasted because it fails to provide the information we need to tell us that one way to teach is that much better than another.

THE NEED FOR ROLE MODELS

Quality schools need quality teachers. If we are willing to accept the ideas of lead-management, much will be accomplished toward reducing the coercion of teachers that is endemic in the present system, and which significantly reduces their effectiveness. But still much more on-the-job training is needed for what I am convinced (see Chapter

Two) is the hardest job there is. To accomplish this we need role models: Nothing less will suffice.

Just as there are stars in every field, there are stars in teaching. But while few star baseball players or virtuoso piano players can teach others to do what they do, it is the essence of star teachers that they could do this superbly given the opportunity. *Stand and Deliver* gives some indication of how star teachers' skills could best be transmitted to others who want to learn: Use the media. Although the movie showed what Escalante did, it did not show how he did it. To show this, we need many hours of high-quality videotapes, made for the express purpose of teaching others to do what worked so well for Escalante. I do not claim that every teacher can learn to do what he did; some of his success is unique to his personality. I am convinced, however, from feedback I have received regarding the effectiveness of counselors I have trained to teach reality therapy, that there is much that can be learned about effective teaching that is not based on personality or unusual aptitude.

Making high-quality videotapes for training is the first suggestion I have made in this book that will cost more money than we spend now, but more than enough money to pay for these needed tapes could be saved by cutting back on expensive mass testing that produces little of value. Thousands of teachers entering the profession each year have not recently seen a great teacher teach and have never in their college preparation even talked about what it is that star teachers do.

There is another reason to videotape great teachers as they teach: The videos could be used to teach directly. Students complain about the boredom of many of their classes, but they never complain of boredom when great teachers are teaching. Done correctly and not overused, videotapes of great teachers could be brought into the classroom and used to teach students. Here again statistics need to be kept on how well this kind of instruction works, and small inexpensive pilot studies could be used to test the process before it is increased in scale.

How would we find the great teachers that we need as models? When I talk to students I caution them not to mention any teacher by name, and they understand why. At times, however, they do slip and mention a teacher, but those they identify are always, in their opinion, great teachers. Just as anyone reading this book knows who the great teachers were who taught him or her, so do students today. Finding great teachers will not be the problem. By far the largest obstacles will be raising the money to make the tapes and getting rid of the professional jealousy that hampers their use.

HOMEWORK IN A QUALITY SCHOOL

Difficult as it may be for both educators and parents to accept, mandatory homework may be the main reason that so many students take schoolwork out of their quality worlds. Even the good students that I interview almost always say homework is what they most dislike about school. Very few claim to do all that is assigned and most admit they do much less. This is supported by the 1989 *Kappan* poll in which 79 percent of the elementary school teachers and 85 percent of the high school teachers complained that students do not complete their assignments. This was the teachers' most frequent complaint, substantially larger than discipline infractions (57 percent), the next most frequent complaint.[3] Based on what I have learned from in-depth student interviews, I believe that students fail to complete homework much more often than classwork.

Deming would say that if 80 percent of the workers will not do what they are asked to do, it is the fault of the system. It is neither the fault of teachers, who are doing what the system tells them to do, nor students who are not working. This is a significant statistic proving that the do-what-we-tell-you-to-do-whether-it-is-satisfying-or-not boss-managed system does not work, yet we continue to pay little attention to the system itself. Students who do not do their homework assignments are routinely punished, usually with low grades and threats of failure. By seventh grade, more than half of the students deal with this coercion by taking schoolwork out of their quality world and do less and less classwork. Mandatory homework that is designed to increase the productivity of the system, in practice, severely reduces it.

In a quality school, the lead-teachers would never lose sight of the fact that managing students so that they keep schoolwork in their quality world is the most important priority of the system. Because they know that formal education is over for students who take schoolwork out of their quality world, the focus is always on quality classwork. Students would be given the time to complete their work in class under the direct supervision and support of their teachers and with the help of each other.

The way to solve the problem of students not doing homework is exactly the opposite of what we do now: Reduce compulsory homework drastically and emphasize the importance of classwork. They expect to work in class. If classwork is satisfying, it will become an important part of their quality worlds. They would be taught to evaluate all their work and would always be given a chance to raise their grades by improving it. They would be encouraged to take their work home to do this and most would.

When we attempt to do what does not work, as we are doing now with compulsory homework, both teachers and students lose respect for the system. Coercion is increased and the opportunity for quality is lost. It is unlikely that we will ever figure out how to persuade many students to do the amount of homework mostly assigned now on any consistent basis. Eighty percent of our teachers are not incompetent and they have yet to figure out how to do this.

Besides encouraging them to work voluntarily at home to improve their grades, there may other ways to persuade students to do homework without making it compulsory. A colleague of mine has suggested that homework should be work that can only be done at home rather than an extension of classwork as most of it is now. For example, assignments in which students are asked to interview their parents, watch a specific program on educational television, do research in the community, volunteer for community service, or practice at home or in the community what is learned in school. To promote creativity and initiative, an assignment might be to figure out what could be done at home that would enrich what is being studied in class.

We spend too much effort trying to force students to read and many learn to hate reading. They may still read grudgingly in school but they refuse to read at home. Since reading is so necessary, an effort might be made to promote it at home by trying to convince students that it is satisfying to turn off the television for a while and read. An assignment might be to have each member of a family find something satisfying in a book, newspaper or magazine and read it out loud to the others. Teachers might suggest that there is even much in comics that is educational. For example, "Doonesbury" is excellent for national problems and "Calvin and Hobbes" and "Peanuts" for relationships. Assignments like these could be stepping-stones for more reading. Teachers who have figured out how to persuade students to enjoy reading at home should make this expertise available; we can all use it.

There are many enjoyable games that involve skills of reasoning, decision making, logic, estimating, and geometry that are also educational. Since very few students do homework on weekends, with parental consent, noncompulsory weekend assignments to play Monopoly, chess, checkers, pool, backgammon as well as card games like casino and cribbage might be valuable. All of these are much more educational than watching television or listening to rock music, especially for young children. Given school support, they might even help somewhat in preventing the boredom that leads to drugs.

THE CURRICULUM

For the first ten years of school, most of the curriculum is compulsory. We "know" what students must learn, and we complain because so few of them are learning it as competently as we would like. Actually, there is little wrong with the curriculum. What is wrong is our inability to persuade more than a small percentage of students to learn it well. As in pressuring for homework, if we pressure students to learn what they do not want to learn, and then punish them with low grades when they do not learn it, they counter by taking schoolwork out of their quality worlds, and we lose them as learners.

Instead of telling students what they need to learn and then losing so many of them in the process, we should separate from the bulk of the curriculum the most obviously important parts and ask students if they will accept learning these components well. For example, the popular media consistently report that only a small percentage of high school graduates can write a good letter. To verify this, at the end of the school year in June 1989, I read the results of this study to an English class at the Apollo School, the school where I consulted and where students' academic achievement was low. I asked the students if they would be willing to learn to write three very good letters:

one asking for information, another giving information, and the third giving an opinion as in a letter to the editor of the local newspaper. As part of my argument, I said that students should be able to write a very good letter or they should not graduate from high school. I said that I would want students with a diploma from the Apollo School to be able to say that this diploma certifies that they can do certain things well, one of them being to write a good letter. We talked over what a good letter would be, and I said that they should be the judge. Asked if they could recognize a good letter, students thought that they could.

Next we discussed what would constitute a good letter. The students mentioned neatness, good grammar, correct spelling and usage, and correct form, typewritten if possible. I suggested that if students had any doubt as to whether they had written a good letter, they could ask their teacher, who would be helping them and for whom they had great respect. But I also said that if there was any disagreement as to what was a good letter, they could choose any educated adult and I would accept this person's judgment. The students all agreed that this was a worthwhile English project, and the English faculty made this a high priority item for the fall of 1989. By Christmas, some students were already writing high-quality letters, the best work they had done in English in years.

What I am trying to say is that we should explain much more than we do now, as we would in a lead-managed school, about why we teach the things we do. Then we should break down what we teach into recognizable parts. In English, for example, this might be writing a good letter, reading a good book, acting out a skit or a play, and learning basic grammar. Then we should ask students if they agree that these definite and understandable components are worth learning. Finally, are they willing to learn them until they know them well? If we present these understandable components as a learning choice, most students will agree to learn them, as did the Apollo students.

As hard as it may be to accept, we have to sell what we believe is worth learning to those we teach, who may be quite skeptical. A reputable salesman does not try to force you to buy a product: He makes it clear why it is to your advantage to buy what he sells. I don't see why educators consider it beneath their professional dignity to do the same. We make a big mistake when we assume that students do not want to learn and that we must force them. Almost all we teach is needed, and most students have some idea that this is so. But like many of us who may want something, they still enjoy a little sell. Choice theory also points out that because of the way we are constructed to function, we all want to feel as if we have some control over what we do. When people try to force us, even if we think it may be for our own good, we tend to rebel.

There is nothing inherently wrong with most of our curriculum. What is wrong is the boss-manager approach we use when we present it to the students. If we cannot figure out how to present what we teach in a way that students will easily see that it is worth making the effort to learn, we should not teach it. More often than not, to try to force learning on the unwilling is to promote ignorance.

CHAPTER NINE

Building a Friendly Workplace

All managers have to deal with absenteeism and low productivity, but teachers are among the few managers who must deal with workers who are disruptive. Disruption, while not common, is extremely difficult to handle, but it is not difficult to prevent, providing the teacher manages so that the disruptive student gets no support from the class. To accomplish this, a lead-teacher avoids doing anything that might lead students to see him or her as an adversary. If they see the teacher as an adversary, they will either continue to disrupt or support a disruption. Even good students who never disrupt may lend tacit support to those who do.

Prevention of disruption was a valuable lesson I learned in the eleven years that I worked in a reform school for delinquent adolescent girls. We succeeded in preventing disruption by establishing an almost totally nonadversarial relationship with the young women there. Those who thought about making trouble rarely started because they knew that they would not get support from the group. They were always looking for this support, and they were used to getting it in other places. What was also very helpful was that we were able to operate with very few rules. Mostly we depended upon creating an atmosphere in which the idea of being courteous prevailed. Courtesy is the core of how a lead-manager deals with workers, which sets an example for everyone.

Courtesy means that you are kind; you listen to what the students have to say; you do not criticize, even when students do something you do not want them to do. There is no putting students down, no sarcasm. It is also important to be careful of your language. Regardless of how profane a student may become, do not respond with profanity. Students do not want you to be profane and they will not respect you if you are.

It is in establishing rules that a major difference between boss-managers and lead-managers becomes apparent. Boss-managers depend on rules; when they are in charge, rules tend to proliferate. Boss-managers accept the cliche that workers do not want to work or that students do not want to learn, and they depend on rules to keep them on task. They do not realize that what workers and students want is satisfying work and that having many rules, with a variety of punishments for breaking them, makes work less satisfying. When rules proliferate, time and effort that should be devoted to work is devoted instead to circumventing the rules. Bosses then figure out more rules because rules are sacred to them and often become more important than the problem the rules were intended to solve.

Lead-managers do not depend on rules. They try to solve problems by managing the operation in a way that makes it apparent to the workers that if they work hard, they will feel good, which means that they will satisfy their needs. The only reason to have a rule is to help this to happen. Lead-managers try to have minimal rules because they know that as soon as they are put in the position of trying to enforce a rule, they risk becoming the adversary of the rule-breaker. Therefore, while lead-managers need to have rules, they try to keep them few and simple. The main effort is to eliminate the unwritten rules, such as "You have to do this" or "You can't do that," that seem to crop up constantly in any work situation.

To establish the rules, the lead-manager holds discussions with the workers, trying to get all concerned to agree on the rule and the need for it before it is put into effect. In school, a lead-teacher should begin the year with a discussion with each class about what rules the students think are needed to get the work done. This will set the stage for the many discussions about quality that must be an ongoing part of the quality school program, which will be explained in the last chapter. The teacher should emphasize that his goal is to help students to learn. All he wants is a minimal set of rules; he does not want to have to police unnecessary rules.

As the students offer rules, try to get them to see that if they are courteous, in most cases the rule will not be needed. Try to reverse what most see as the teacher's usual role. You are pushing for fewer rules, not more. After you get these rules, tell students that you can always meet again if a situation arises where an additional rule is needed. Then go on to the critical part of the discussion: What should be done when a rule is broken? Students will tell you to punish, as this is the only approach to enforcing rules they know.

Explain carefully that they, not you, are suggesting punishment. You neither believe in it nor want to punish when a rule is broken. Students will begin to get the idea that you are not the usual boss-teacher, and my experience is that they become very interested at this point. Ask them if they think punishment works. Be specific by asking, "Does it work with you?" Although they have just recommended it, most will say that it does not work.

To help students with this dilemma ask, "Do you think the student who breaks the rules usually has some kind of problem?" In all cases they will say, "Yes." Then ask them what is the best approach to a problem. In fact, push them a little further and ask, "What is the only approach to a problem?" Their answer will be, "Solve it." Tell them that this is exactly what you want to do. Then ask, "How do you solve a problem?" or more specifically, "What does each person who is part of the problem have to do?" Here, what-ever they say, you should summarize by suggesting that all the people involved have to work on the problem.

Ask students if the people who have the problem can continue to do the same thing that they were doing when the problem occurred. When students say that they can't, try to come up with a typical problem, such as a student who is frequently late for class, and ask how they suggest you and the student solve this problem without punish-ment. Mostly they will not know what to do: It has never occurred to them that problems like these can be solved without punishment.

Keep insisting, however, and remind them that not only the student, but also the teacher may need to do something different. Ask, "What could I do?" Eventually, they may suggest that you talk to the student and try to make the student feel more welcome in class, or help the student to figure out how to do better, or maybe listen to a personal problem the student is struggling with that has little to do with school. Try to help students to see that your giving time and attention to an area far removed from the pre-senting problem could be the key to its solution.

See if students agree that if you give a little, the student will give a little also. Point out how different this is from punishment, and ask them if this approach makes sense.

This will help you to become more of a leader and much less of a boss.

Once you have a set of rules, write the rules down. Then have all class members sign a paper attesting that they have read the rules and that if they break them, they will try, with your help, to solve the underlying problem. Remind them that the rules are not written in stone: If another rule is needed or any rule does not seem to be working, you are open to their suggestions and you expect that they will also be open to yours.

Lay some groundwork for students to follow the rules by admitting that your class is no different from most classes in that some of the material you will ask them to learn will be boring. But also tell them that when things get boring, you are willing to work with them to try to find a more interesting way to teach the material. What you are doing is preparing students to accept some alternative ways to teach, such as cooperative learning. They will be more willing to try new ways if they are involved with you in figuring them out. Be sure to tell them that they are lucky: Most of what you teach they have to learn only once; you have to teach it "forever."

From the beginning, show interest in students' personal lives and reveal some facts about your life and some experiences you have had that may intrigue them. To avoid subjects that may be too personal, I suggest following a simple rule: Never ask anyone anything about his or her life that you are not prepared to reveal about your own. Most students are not on easy personal terms with adults, in many cases not even their own parents. Sharing small parts of your life, especially little problems and some of your foolishness, will lead students to become closer and more supportive of you. The more they know you and understand some of your struggles, the more they will tend to be on your side. Not knowing another person, especially one who has power over you as a teacher does over a student, makes anyone more likely to cast that person in the role of an adversary or, at least, not as a friend.

Ask for students' help and advice in any way that you can. Don't struggle by yourself with anything that they could conceivably help you with. Nothing gives students more of a sense of power than advising the teacher, and the more they can help you by doing something that you seem unable to do for yourself, the more important they will feel. For example, ask them about how to deal with friends and neighbors, what to buy, where to go, and what to do. It doesn't matter that you may not take their advice, ask anyway. If you do take some advice, try to let the whole class know that you learned something from them.

It may seem that what I have just suggested would take a great deal of time, but it need not. You should try to keep interjecting a few personal asides for a few seconds here and there as you teach. Keep a dialogue going with students about anything: The more you and they talk, even if it is just for a few seconds, the more accepted you will be and the less they will see you as an adversary. Friendly, easy conversation is the most important defense against being seen as a boss. You will convey the message that you want to be followed not because it is good for you, but because it is good for them. By accomplishing this early in the school year, you lay the groundwork for establishing not only that you are not their adversary, but that you are their friend.

In choice theory terms, what I have been suggesting in this chapter will enable your students to put you into their quality worlds as a need-satisfying friend. Once there, most of your problems as a teacher will disappear. If you are not able to get into students' quality worlds, it is unlikely that they will do much quality work.

Traditionally, bosses are admonished that they should not be friendly with workers. Where threats and punishment are the main way to "motivate," this is easy advice to follow. Those who give this advice believe in punishment and know that it is hard to punish a friend. They also fear that the weaker friend may try to take advantage of the friendship, and the power of the boss will be compromised.

Empowering the workers is not as easy as it would seem because workers, especially workers who have been boss-managed, are leery of power. They recognize that with it comes increased responsibility. As long as they accept that the manager has all the power, the workers can blame the manager when things go wrong, and they usually do. When the workers have power, they have to work harder or more carefully because now they, along with the manager, are responsible for what is produced.

When lead-managers offer workers more power by stopping punishment, talking over problems, and listening to their solutions, many workers may think at first that they are being manipulated to get them to work harder. But lead-managers use more pay, more personal attention, and more say in what goes on in the workplace as tangible means to convince workers that what they are doing is for their own benefit. Although better grades are the equivalent in school of more pay, more attention and more say-so are perhaps even more important than in industry.

If lead-managers succeed in ridding themselves of the boss image and the quality of the work goes up, then it becomes easy to be friends with those they manage. Everyone shares in the success, cooperation increases, power struggles end, and the whole issue of power melts away. Lead-managers are much different from boss-managers in that they recognize that the manager's main concern should be quality, not power. Lead-managers are well aware that power struggles are the main enemy of quality.

As lead-teachers succeed in shedding the power image and becoming friends with students, more students feel empowered. They work harder and become friendlier with the teacher, and both students and teacher feel better. What finally happens is that the quality of the work becomes very high, everyone feels more powerful, and the craving for power for the sake of power, which is so detrimental to production, becomes unnecessary.

Teachers have an advantage over industrial managers in that friendship between them and good students is traditional and, therefore, more acceptable than friendships in the industrial workplace. So the previous suggestions, equally applicable to school and industry, are easier to accomplish in school. There is a long history of strong friendships, even love, between teacher and student, and much student success is based on this closeness. Annie Sullivan was a loving friend to Helen Keller, and the fictional Mr. Chips was a dear friend to his students.

There is not a person reading these words who has not been befriended by a teacher and who did not benefit from that friendship. My own life was turned around by a teacher in graduate school who asked me what plans I had for the future. This brief conversation was the first time since elementary school that anyone in any school had taken a personal interest in me, and from it I was empowered to try to enter medical school which, because of low grades in undergraduate school, I had thought impossible. Between a teacher and a student, a little friendly interest goes a long way.

Past elementary school, more than half of all students are friends neither with their teacher nor with the students who are doing well in their classes. Not only do they not see the teacher as their friend, but even worse they see the teacher as an adversary. They do have friends in school, but these friends are also allies in their struggle against the unfriendly, boss-managed education they are being offered. This struggle produces the low-quality education that we have.

While these students would be worse off if they had no friends at all, it is unlikely that they will be productive until they believe that they can be friends with their teachers and with the students who now do well in class. These friendships alone may not be enough to get them to work hard, but without them, nothing else suggested in this book will make much difference. Eliminating the adversarial relationships is a good start, but replacing them with friendships is basic to solving our educational problems.

VOLUNTEER "FRIENDS"

I am frequently asked how to deal with the very few students whose behavior is so totally disruptive that it is almost impossible for their teachers to teach effectively. My observation is that, unlike other disruptive students who have friends and are willing to accept friendship from the teacher, these students have almost no friends in school. Driven to desperation by their need for friendship and recognition, they are unpredictably disruptive. Even a competent lead-teacher does not have the time to give them what they need if they are to be reached.

In my opinion, these students need more personal attention in school than it is possible for the staff to give them. They need adults who have the capacity to approach them in such a warm and friendly way that they will be accepted as friends. The best help, and from a practical standpoint the only help, is to use adult volunteer "friends." Senior citizens are especially useful here, and school administrators who are good lead-managers will make it a part of their jobs to reach out to the community and recruit adult "friends" to help with these angry or withdrawn students.

The volunteer "friend" will demonstrate his or her friendship by spending time with the lonely student. What they do together need satisfy only one criterion, that they both enjoy spending this time with each other. Until they are good friends, there should be no other agenda. It should be recognized that unless such students have a friend, they will not function. These students have absorbed a great deal of punishment from a series of bosses in and out of school, and this destructive cycle is best broken by friendship with a successful adult.

What the volunteers do is specifically designed to help the students to satisfy their needs, especially the need to belong and the need for power. As this is accomplished, the students make the crucial discovery that they are happier because of something the school has provided and begin to consider moving the picture of school back into their quality worlds. Unless this occurs, the students will get little benefit from school. The volunteers must spend time with the students on a regular basis. It need be a significant amount of time, usually at least two hours a week. With this much help, most students will begin to work in school, and the volunteers can offer to tutor because these students are usually far behind. Some of them, however, are quite capable. They can do the work and need only the friendly support of the volunteer to get enough need-satisfaction to begin.

Most schools have a tradition of using volunteers to help in a variety of ways, but having volunteers befriend students and serve as mentors to them, as suggested here, is a new idea for many schools.[1] In most cases, the students they help will be difficult to get along with in the beginning. Many will be abrasive, some despondent, and almost all self-destructive. My suggestion is to start with only a few volunteers recruited from interested friends, perhaps no more than three, and give this initial group training and support. As they become skilled and spread the word that they enjoy what they are doing, they will recruit any additional help that may be needed.

STUDENT PEER COUNSELORS

Volunteers should not be limited to adults. Students should also be involved. There are a wide variety of ways in which students can help each other, from tutoring to counseling. One of the best programs is to train student volunteers to act as peer counselors. When a student with a problem is counseled by a trained peer, both are well served. The counselor gains from learning the skills to help others, and the counselee gains from the counseling and also from being exposed to the role model of the successful student who does the counseling.

The student peer counselors should always be available during the same day they are requested, and all students who will accept counseling from their peers should be given this opportunity. Because this takes time away from other things that the student counselor might do, there should always be enough students trained so that no one student will be overloaded with this responsibility. A professional school counselor or administrator should be in charge of the program and should provide regular supervision for the student counselors. Together, they should make decisions as to whether the student being counseled needs more help, more time, or whatever.

It is beyond the scope of this chapter to spell out further how to increase the friendliness of the school. I am sure that experienced teachers could add many ideas to the few I have outlined here. What I am trying to do is to emphasize that in a quality school, no student will be able to say, "No one cares." In fact, it should be hard for any student to say that only a few people care because almost everyone will be friendly and helpful.

The main concern of lead-managers is to provide a workplace in which the workers can satisfy their needs, understanding that all work, including schoolwork, is rarely consistently satisfying. But if the workplace is satisfying, it can usually more than make up for what is lacking in the work itself. What will satisfy an unhappy worker is the observation that the manager is trying to make the workplace satisfying. This is often sufficient to keep the worker going through a difficult time. In temporarily unsatisfying situations, most workers will recognize the limitations that the manager is struggling with. In the case of school, most students will accept that there are subjects that are very difficult to make exciting.

What the students want is a school where it is apparent to all that the staff is constantly trying to make things better. This strong, "We care" message is the foundation of quality education.

CHAPTER TEN

Dealing with Discipline Problems

Several years ago I worked with corporate executives, essentially boss-managers, who were trying to learn better ways to deal with problem employees. They complained about lateness, absenteeism, substandard work, and the inability to work with others, but these problems involved only a few of the people they managed. They never faced the insubordination, total lack of effort, and noncaring attitude that boss-teachers face every day with up to half of their students. While business managers would benefit by changing to lead-management to deal more effectively with problem workers, such a change is essential for teachers.

All managers, lead or boss, find insubordination hard to accept. Both types of managers believe that workers should accept the conditions of the job (or school) and do as they are told, but lead-managers differ greatly from boss-managers in how they deal with the problem of uncooperative workers: They never coerce; they make an effort to talk to workers about their grievances, and they are open to suggestions on how working conditions might be improved.

In industry, a worker who is grossly insubordinate is threatened with discharge. If the worker continues to cause trouble, he is almost certain to be fired. Insubordination is not tolerated. When students are disruptive or nonworking, most teachers also look for a boss approach that is quick and decisive. They want something simple to do that will get the problem quickly under control. Many would love it if they could fire the student, but unfortunately even disruptive students have "tenure" and are almost impossible to get rid of.

When disruption occurs in school, it is usually with students who have had great difficulty satisfying their needs in school. As a result, they have very few pictures of school, schoolwork, or teachers in their quality worlds. When these students sit in class, at any moment the difference between whatever it is they may want and what they have may become extreme. Pushed by this difference, their attitude is an angry, confrontational one: "I don't care what you do, I am not going to sit down and pay attention." What is so hard for boss-teachers to face is that there is nothing they can do at that tense moment that will be effective.

Kicking disruptive students out of class, keeping them after school in detention, or suspending them may control the immediate situation, but it does not deal with the basic problem: how to get them involved in quality learning. In the quality school, lead-teachers must learn how to handle a disruptive student in a way that is not punitive yet gets the situation under control and, at the same time, opens the student's mind to the option of beginning to work in class.

Among the first thoughts that cross most teachers' minds is to call the student's home, but this rarely works the way it is intended. Boss-teachers who do this want the parent to punish the child for what he or she has done in class, and too many parents, also boss-managers, are more than willing to do so. Students do not like to be punished in any case, and in this case the student correctly sees the school as the cause of the trouble he or she now has at home. This common practice thus tends to compound many more problems than it solves.

Lead-teachers try very hard to deal with a disruptive student without notifying the parents. In fact, I believe that, as a general rule, the school should notify parents only to tell them positive things about their child. As much as possible, discipline problems should be dealt with when they occur without involving parents. This says to the disruptive student, "We believe you are capable of working out your problems without getting your parents involved."

This message also strongly says, "We want to solve the problem, not punish you, and we are not looking for a way to get your parents to punish you," which is what many students believe is the main reason teachers contact parents. Calling in the parents is also an admission that the school cannot handle its own problems, an admission that managers should not make.

Sometimes, however, parents are called to discuss problems that have nothing to do with discipline. The student may be having trouble making friends, for example. When a conference with parents is necessary, the student should be present and the lead-teacher should make clear that the student is not doing anything wrong and that the purpose of the conference is not to get the student punished at home. The goal is to involve the parents in a nonpunitive plan to help their child do better in school.

Good advice for parents who are called in to school for any reason is for one or both to spend more time doing things with the child that both the child and the parents enjoy. It is especially important that the parent who is with the child the least, usually the father, spend this quality time. Some students disrupt in school hoping that the parent they do not see enough of will get involved, because even negative attention from this parent is better than the small amount of attention they now receive. If there is no father or male in the home, as is often the case, then the school should encourage the mother to have a male relative or friend spend some time with the student.

DEALING EFFECTIVELY WITH DISRUPTIVE STUDENTS

Suppose that you have begun to convert from boss-managing to lead-managing. You have stopped punishing, you are doing your best to model and facilitate in an effort to improve classroom conditions, and you have worked out a set of rules with your students that they have agreed to follow. You have the needs of your students in mind and are trying to run your class in a way that is satisfying for all.

There are, however, still occasional problems with students who, while not grossly insubordinate, refuse to settle down to work as quickly and quietly as you would like. You know that these students are not lonely and that they are capable of doing good work, but today one of them is choosing to ignore the rules enough so that you must deal with him. Although the class is not supportive, they are watching and you have the distinct impression that they are casting you back into the boss-manager role you are trying so hard to get away from. Unlike boss-managers, lead-managers should be able to deal with any disruptive students effectively.

In what follows in this chapter, it is assumed that for the first several years, as it changes from boss-management to lead-management, the quality school will have a time-out room to which a disruptive student can be sent. Without such a room, disruptive students cannot usually be counseled successfully. As I am well aware that teachers with classes of more than thirty students have little time to deal with problems, none of the following suggestions takes more than twenty seconds of class time. But no matter how busy you may be, these few seconds are well spent. To do less is to make the problem, whatever it may be, more difficult to solve.

The lead-teacher is aware that he has no magic, no quick fix to solve problems. He must communicate to the student clearly that not only does he have no magic, but he needs no magic. The lead-teacher communicates this by dealing with all infractions in essentially the same matter-of-fact way. Because it is always the same, the student will get the message that his particular insubordination is no big deal and that the teacher has confidence in what he, the teacher, is doing. It also tells the student that his disruption is his problem, not the teacher's: the teacher knows what to do.

The lead-manager teacher should always say something like the following to the disruptive student:

> It looks like you have a problem. How could I help you solve it? If you'll just calm down, as soon as I have the time, I'll talk it over with you and I think we can work something out. As long as you're doing what you're doing now, we can't work anything out.

Tailor what I suggest to your own style: I am sure that many of you could say it in fewer words. You could also add gestures, a shrug of your shoulders, or an extension of your hands to take the place of many words. However you do it, you are making it clear that you will not help the student to work out the problem until he cools off. A lead-teacher will do this calmly. There is no reason to get angry or be put on the defensive by one disruptive student. If most of the class is satisfied, any disruption will be only a little brush fire, never a big blaze.

If the teacher can joke a little while asking the student to calm down, so much the better. A joke cuts the tension and works best when it is at the teacher's expense or exaggerates the problem. The fact that the teacher had the confidence to make this kind of joke is a show of strength, never weakness. Although the teacher can put himself down a little, he should never put the student down. Perhaps the teacher could say in a mock serious tone:

> Wow, you're upset. I must be doing something really terrible. Calm down, and as soon as I can, we'll get together and maybe you can help me work things out.

Said with a smile and an appropriate gesture, this may break the tension and "allow" the student to sit down because he knows he has made his point. Getting the immediate situation under control is the way to begin dealing with any disruption.

If the student will not calm down after this reasonable request, there is no good way to deal with him in class. Some ways are better than others, however, including never getting into an argument or even a long discussion with an angry student about the merits of his case. Above all, do not threaten. Just do what has been suggested and if the student will not calm down in the twenty seconds that I suggest should be allotted, ask him to leave the class. (What should be done with the student when he leaves the class will be covered in detail shortly.) Keep in mind that the vast majority of disruptive students who do not have the tacit or active support of their classmates, if dealt with as I have suggested, will calm down in twenty seconds. There is nothing better that can be done at that tense moment; anything else will usually be worse.

All the students, including the one who has just dis-
rupted, should hear the message that lead-managers do not
threaten. They recognize that there are problems and try to
solve them, but they cannot solve them by themselves.
They need the cooperation of the student. If the student
will not cooperate and must be asked to leave the room,
the teacher should say something like this:

> Since you won't calm down, I have to ask you to leave. I
> hope we can get together later and work this out, but if
> you are not willing to settle down, it's better that you
> leave now.

This way the door is kept open, and there are no threats
or hassles. The disruptive student is looking for someone
to blame in order to justify keeping his grievance alive. But
it's hard to stay angry at a teacher who is saying, both in
words and demeanor:

> I want to help you work this out. I am not looking to
> punish you for what you have just done. If there is a
> problem, let's solve it.

Teachers who are used to the boss approach may find it
difficult to accept that there is nothing effective that can be
done immediately. The teacher can only set the stage for
solving the problem later when both are calm. The ultimate goal is to get the disruptive student to start working.
Even if a threat gets the student to quiet down, it does not
get him to think about changing what he is doing in
school.

Only when teachers stop looking for what has never
existed—quick fixes—will they begin to accept that the
only good solutions to discipline problems are systematic
and long-term. Long-term solutions to problems, no mat-

ter how serious, must be developed while the student is not disruptive. Problems can never be solved in the heat of anger, so the lead-teacher focuses first on calming the immediate situation.

If the student calms down in class, you need to find a time to talk to him. This may be in class, between classes, before or after school, or any time you can spare a few minutes. If you need more than five minutes, you will have to arrange a special time. A minute or two should be enough to deal with most cases, however, except those that are so severe that you need to involve a counselor or an administrator. When you have the time, what you say should always be about the same as the following:

> What were you doing when the problem started? Was this against the rules? Can we work it out so that it doesn't happen again? If this situation comes up in the future, let's work out what you could do and what I could do so we don't have this problem again.

In this way you are solving the problem by giving the attention that the student wants and may also need. If you are wise, you will try to give him a little extra attention in the ongoing dialogue that I have suggested be a part of what you do regularly when you teach. But because you are now running a need-satisfying class, most of the time you will not have to work anything out. Once the student calms down, he'll probably agree that it won't happen again.

The vast majority of disruptive students you will have to deal with will not have big problems. Once they cool off, they usually do not want to go through a lengthy discussion about their temporary foolishness. But if a student is having trouble with another student, you may have to talk to one or both students to work out a way that they can get along better. You would handle this situation the same way:

What were you [first student] doing? What were you [second student] doing? How could each of you [address each student] do something different that would prevent this from happening again?

Do not spend time trying to find out whose fault it is. Just tell the students involved that each has a problem to solve and that they can work on it separately or together, depending on which they prefer. Tell them that your goal is to help them to get along better and to do well in school. You are not looking for whose fault it is, just for a solution.

Obviously, the student or students may not be as cooperative as I have described, but this should not change your approach. No matter what students do, stick to getting the facts on the table: What was done was against the rules. You should insist that students focus on what they can do to prevent this problem in the future. It doesn't matter if the students do not come up with an exact plan; what matters is that you insist that there's a way to solve the problem. And if the disruptive students see you as a leader who cares, not as a boss who punishes, they will usually figure out a way to follow the rules.

Students will soon discover that you have given them every chance. If they want to stay in class, they have no choice but to follow the rules, at least until you talk things over. And if your students are satisfied most of the time, they'll want to stay. If a student calms down and seems satisfied, keep in mind that he may still have a problem that could be helped by talking to him, but this is not the time to attempt to do this. Wait a while, maybe a few days. Try to find a time when the student has enjoyed a little success in class, and then ask him if he would like to have a chat about how he is doing. If he opens up to you, just listen. Compliment him on doing better in class, tell him that you have enjoyed your little talk, and suggest that the two of you get together again for a talk. The student will probably agree to this suggestion. If you follow through, it is unlikely that you will have much trouble with him in the future. While this may sound like a lot of work, teachers who do it report that it is very pleasant and gives a real sense of satisfaction to their jobs.

Too often managers tend to manage by the "leave-well-enough-alone" philosophy, but "well enough" will not be good enough unless there is an ongoing effort to make the workplace satisfying for everyone. Therefore, the lead-manager is constantly trying to see that small problems are solved before they become large ones. Taking a little time to listen to a student who is a potential troublemaker is part of being a good lead-teacher.

What this accomplishes is that students, who see you always trying to make the classroom a better place to learn, try to solve many of their own problems and often help each other. They recognize that a little effort on their part is necessary if they are to keep the good situation that they have. If students do not see that you are making this effort, they will let you take over when problems occur; after all, "you're the boss." Don't be the boss: Talk to your students and be a problem solver, and fewer problems will occur.

DEALING WITH STUDENTS WHO ARE ASKED TO LEAVE THE CLASS

Whether it happens early in elementary school or in the last part of high school, the first time a student disrupts enough to be asked to leave the class is a crucial point in that student's school career. If this situation is dealt with well, it may be the last time he disrupts to this extent, but once it becomes a chronic problem where he is kicked out of class over and over, it becomes almost impossible to solve.

Whether it is an administrator or a counselor who deals with the student who is sent from class, the lead-manager approach should be continued. Concede that there is a problem, maybe even be a big one, but you will try to help the student solve it. There should be no threats or punishment, no semblance of the usual boss-manager approach that the student may expect. If, however, the student has been exposed to a lead-managed school, he will not expect punishment and will already be amenable to the problem-solving approach that is the only one that will work in the long run. Just because it did not work in the classroom does not mean that it will not work. If it is used consistently both in and out of class, it will work eventually, in one place or another.

Do not be misled into thinking that because the problem-solving lead-manager approach is nonpunitive, it is soft. It is really the toughest approach of all because the student has to take some responsibility for solving the problem instead of letting the boss do it all. This approach can involve restricting the student to a "time-out" room, a restriction that should be continued until he is willing to start working on the problem. A time-out room is just a room in the school run by someone who has experience dealing with students who have been asked to leave class. If the school is lead-managed, no matter how large the school, there will rarely be more than a few students in the room.

In a lead-managed school, there are almost no disruptive students and no need for a time-out room. When a problem occurs, the student is always ready to work to solve it. As a school begins the move to becoming a quality school, the need for a time-out room begins to diminish, so what I am talking about here is only temporary. When the transition to a quality school is complete—this should take no more than four years—there should be no discipline problems serious enough to require a time-out room.

It usually does not take more than an hour or two to get a solution started, but the student should remain in the time-out room even if it takes much longer. The student may protest that it is unfair and that you are punishing him by keeping him there, but you have to point out that it is his choice not to begin to work to solve the problem. As soon as he starts working on a solution, he can go back to class.

You should also point out that in the time-out room he not only has a chance to do his schoolwork, but he may even get some help so that he can keep up with the class. He is always treated with courtesy and offered counseling. The student's parents should not be involved unless he starts to fall behind in his classwork. He should be constantly reminded that no one wants him to stay in restriction: Everyone wants him to begin to work on the problem and will help in any way possible. The student should be told over and over, and as kindly as possible, that it is his choice to be there and that only he can make a better choice.

In the time-out room the only rule is that the students sit quietly. They are encouraged to do their work, but if they just want to sit, that is their privilege. If the person running the time-out room judges this to be beneficial, students may be allowed to work together as long as they are not just socializing. The teacher or counselor running this room may also involve the students in a discussion of how they can solve their problems, but this is optional. The main thing is that this room be seen as an opportunity to solve a problem, not as punishment, and that the person in charge is a friend trying to help, not a boss trying to throw his weight around.

When counseling in the time-out room, the counselor should be prepared to deal with the following common complaints:

1. The teacher doesn't like me.
2. The class is boring.
3. I don't need this class for anything that I want to do with my life.

While the whole staff should constantly work to make the school a better place, this is not the time to apologize for what the student thinks is wrong with the school. Agree with him if he says the teacher does not like him and that the class may be boring. Point out that the teacher is not a saint and that no one likes a person who makes trouble. If he finds the class boring, is being in the time-out room better? Don't argue about whether or not he needs what is taught in the class, but ask whether he needs this particular class to graduate. If this is acceptable policy in your school, you might tell him, "If you are willing to do enough work to get to the point where you are in good standing in this class, I will consider changing you to a different class, but I will not change you as long as you are doing poor work." Some schools have a no-change policy to prevent too much student movement, and for these schools this suggestion would not apply.

The purpose of doing this is to show the student that slacking off is his choice, but it is not a way to escape from responsibility. If he starts to work, it is likely that he will find the class less boring than when he was not working and also that the teacher may begin to like him. After that, this class may seem as good as any other class he might move to. Besides, in this class he does not have to start over.

The important thing is not to argue with the student. You will not convince him, and he will enjoy the fact that you are arguing for a lost cause. Your position should not be based on how good you think any class or teacher is or how bad the student may think one or both of these may be. It should be based on the fact that this is the best school that you can offer him right now and that everyone is working to make it better. If he continues to argue that the school has shortcomings, you should ask, "What can you do to make it better?"

As you counsel, be warm and friendly. Do not make the student's problem into a big deal. Imply or say flatly that what he is struggling with is solvable but that he has to do something different in order to solve it. To make this point, go through what he did in class to get removed. Ask him if what he did was against the rules, which of course it was, and then tell him that he should be prepared to stay in the time-out room until he works out a better way: There is no other choice. Remind the student that the length of stay is up to him. It is not that hard to work out a plan to get back to class, and you don't want him to spend a long time in the room.

Be sure to point out to him (if it is true, and it should be true if the school has switched to lead-management) that he has little support from the class for what he did to get removed and even less for the time he is spending in this time-out room. Ask him to ask his friends if they think it is smart to stay in this room instead of trying to make a plan to get out. The point you are trying to make is that a class led by a lead-teacher will not support a disruptive student by giving him a great deal of attention. This lack of support is crucial to the success of this program.

As you work out a plan for the student to do something better, make sure he understands that it is not that hard to follow the rules because almost all the students (in a lead-managed school) do. Then take the further step of trying to work out a way to get the student and the teacher on better terms. Tell him that the plan will work best if the teacher who asked him to leave is able to see that he is doing something tangible to be a better student. If he is willing to try, ask the teacher to make some sort of a small, special effort to express appreciation that the student is trying.

Try to get the student back to class as soon as possible, but do not rush him back so quickly that he does not have time to realize that he should be thinking of something better to do. Also keep in mind that the student should stay out of class long enough so that the teacher does not think he went through a revolving door. The amount of time the student stays in this room should not be related to the degree of disturbance, but to his willingness to try to find a way to correct what he did wrong in class.

What I have just described should be the only disciplinary approach used in a quality school. Do the same thing over and over. Use the time-out room for all problems of disruption. Do not use this room for problems that do not involve disruption, such as not working in class. These are educational, not discipline, problems and can be solved only by counseling, usually by the lead-teacher herself. Taking the nondisruptive, nonworker out of any class only makes the problem worse. He, more than anyone, needs to be in class. The argument that his nonwork will be contagious is not valid. Students do not avoid work because of what others do; they avoid it when they fail to find it satisfying.

Obviously the person in charge of the time-out room should have training and time to work with students. This is a job for a school counselor, but, at present, few school counselors can take the time to sit in a room with only a few students. This may be another job for volunteers; in some schools it has been handled competently by parents or senior citizens.[1]

Keep in mind that all of the ideas suggested in this chapter and the previous one will work well only if the students see their school as a place where they can satisfy their needs. This is always the goal of lead-management.

CHAPTER ELEVEN

Creating the Quality School

In July 1989, I was approached by the superintendent of a small (grades 9 to 12) school district in central California who told me that he had read some material on the quality school, and wanted to move his school in that direction. Whether or not this school followed through and became a quality school, what we worked out could serve as a start-up model for any school that wants to move in this direction.

We began with a meeting in which he and his top administrators agreed to gradually involve all of the staff in choice theory and reality therapy training. This would start with the top managers taking a week's training during the school year. For reasons I will shortly explain, I do not believe that any school will be able to complete the move to a quality school until all the administrators and a majority of the teachers have at least two one-week training sessions in these basic concepts.

The superintendent, however, asked me if it would be possible to begin the program in September before anyone began formal training. He felt, and I agreed, that if they had to wait until everyone was trained in the theory and practice, a process that takes several years, they might lose interest long before much was accomplished. As important as it is, the formal training is not the first thing to do when an administrator decides to try to move to a lead-managed, quality school.

What the person in charge has to do is present the ideas in the first chapter of this book to teachers and show them that he is serious by beginning to use lead-management when he makes this presentation. Teachers will not be interested unless they see immediately that they, as well as their students, are to get the benefit of this new way to manage. Starting in that meeting and continuing unchanged throughout the whole process, the message from the top to the staff must be, "How can we help you much more than we have helped you in the past?"

In schools where the present management is considering making this move, the managers are very likely to be on good terms with the teachers. Still it would be unusual for the teachers to see management, friendly as it may be, as a direct source of help. There is a big difference between a benevolent boss and an actively helping and facilitating leader, and the best way to make this difference clear is to ask at this first meeting for suggestions from the teachers as to how management could help them to teach more effectively.

The teachers will be wary of this new approach, as most low-level managers are when the boss tells them that things are going to be better. The first thought that will go through their minds will probably be: "This is another half-baked scheme that isn't going to work. It's going to make a lot more work for us, and we have too much already." It isn't necessary to address this attitude, but it is necessary to know that it is there as it will tend to limit the suggestions the teachers will offer. It may be that very few will be offered, but all of them should be carefully written down. This initial reluctance to go on record is also to avoid being seen by the boss as a complainer and will dissipate when the teachers find as the program develops that their job is actually better. Skeptical as they will be, asking them what they want that they do not have is a very good way to start.

If I were running this meeting, I would address the universal complaint of good teachers that boss-managers rarely address: Teachers are locked into the classroom, and administrators and other out-of-classroom personnel have no appreciation for how little free time a teacher has during the day for research, preparation, and counseling students. I would also address the corollary complaint, which is that once a teacher moves to an out-of-classroom job, whether it is as a consultant, counselor, or administrator, he or she tends to forget how locked-in teachers are.

A very effective way to reduce the initial skepticism is to present a way in which lead-management would begin immediately to deal with both these real issues. As the teachers agree that they would like more out-of-class time, the administrator running this first meeting should suggest getting together with a committee of teachers to work out how this and other problems could be solved. He might add that one way this could be accomplished would be for out-of-classroom personnel to spend more time in class relieving teachers so that they are less locked-in. This offer to work out problems through committees, which always include people who have the power to solve the problems, is the heart of lead-management.

The specifics of the plan would have to be worked out in committee, but I recommend that the wide gap between those who teach and the administrators and consultants who do not be drastically narrowed in a quality school. All out-of-classroom personnel, even including the superintendent, should teach on a regular basis at least one hour a week and up to several hours a day when possible. In most schools, there are enough able teachers not teaching now so that in time, with the additional help of volunteers and student assistants, it might not be unrealistic for all teachers to have an extra hour each day of classroom free time in addition to what they have now. This would show that the out-of-classroom personnel appreciate what teachers do and would lead to a better feeling between the two groups, which is a goal of lead-management.

After this initial meeting in which the administration declares its desire to move to a quality school, the teachers should be asked if they would be willing to spend more time after school begins in staff meetings for the purpose of learning more about what constitutes a quality school. There is enough material in this book to get any interested teacher well acquainted with these ideas even before formal training begins. (The sooner it can begin, however, the better.)

Assuming that there is initial interest, the first three chapters of this book should be made available on a chapter-by-chapter basis to all faculty and discussed in meetings led by an administrator familiar with the whole book. After the staff has gone carefully through these three chapters, teachers would have enough information to make a preliminary decision as to whether they wanted to get involved in a specific program aimed at moving the school to a quality school. The administration would already have shown their good faith by forming the committee working on utilizing out-of-classroom personnel in the classroom, and this should encourage teachers to choose to get involved.

If at least half the faculty were interested after reviewing and discussing all the implications in the first three chapters, there would be sufficient numbers to move further. If not, I do not think it would be worth making the effort, and the school should wait until there are enough models around so that the value of these ideas is obvious.

Once this preliminary commitment is made, I suggest that all interested teachers agree to spend the first school year going through the rest of the book systematically to understand the ideas well enough to test them in their classes during this first year. Uncommitted teachers would be encouraged to attend these meetings. but, following lead-management, attendance would be optional. By the end of the school year, the administration would be ready for the second week of training, and teachers who could work it into their schedules would take the first week.

Assuming there was interest at the initial meeting, the first step would be for the administration to write a purpose for the school because, if an organization is to achieve quality, Deming insists that top management begin by clearly and succinctly defining the organization's purpose. After this is done, the administration would need to consult with the teachers who were interested after reading and discussing the first three chapters to find out if they accept this statement of purpose. While quality schools may differ slightly in what they see as their purpose, I doubt if any school that does not agree to the following will be able to make the move to quality:

> All students should achieve a level of competence in all courses they attempt that both they and their teachers agree is quality education.

This purpose is stated in very general terms because, as Deming explains, to be specific here is not desirable. To set precise standards or goals for what is to be accomplished is to risk limiting the productivity to that standard. For example, if both faculty and students agree that one of the tasks of a quality school is to teach all the students to write a quality letter, there should never be an exact definition of what this is. No matter how well students write, they may still be able to do better. To quote Deming, "Improve constantly and forever the system of production and service."[1]

If either the teacher or the student decides that a submitted letter is not quality, the student should work until both decide it is. If they have trouble deciding, they should get another opinion. In a quality school, however, it is accepted that quality can be recognized and that people can usually agree that it is present. But it is also accepted that it need not be defined and that, good as it may become, it can always be improved.

TRAINING IN CHOICE THEORY

Once the purpose is set, the part of the staff that agrees to this purpose and wants to start the move to a quality school must become highly conversant with the concepts of choice theory and reality therapy. Teachers will not move to lead-management unless they are more than just acquainted with the choice theory that explains the needs, the quality world, and the way we behave. They must know it well enough so that they use it in their lives, and this takes time and at least two weeks of formal training. To attempt to move a school to the point where all the students are involved in quality work without this training would be more difficult than learning to fly an airplane from an instruction manual.

It takes a working knowledge of choice theory for teachers to accept that the students in their classes who are not working hard have not yet figured out how to satisfy their needs in these classes. Without enough training to use choice theory in their lives, teachers will tend to continue to believe that they can make students work. Training is necessary because even the smallest amount of this coercive, boss attitude will taint the atmosphere and prevent any school from becoming a quality school.

Training in reality therapy, the method of counseling I have been teaching for years that is based completely on choice theory, is also necessary. Teachers who take this training learn how to talk to students, especially to the nonworking students, without using coercion. For most teachers, the complete elimination of coercion is a new experience, and if they do not learn how to do it, they will fail to become lead-teachers. In this context, reality therapy is far more than a method of counseling; it is a noncoercive method of talking to people that managers need to learn to be successful. As managers grow skilled in this noncoercive way to deal with workers, they will be able to persuade workers to begin to take responsibility for what they do and, at the same time, prevent them from believing that they are being pushed by a manager to do what they do not want to do.

Extensive training in a combination of reality therapy and choice theory is available through the William Glasser Institute.² Staff at the schools that have had this training are using what they learned to manage teachers as well as students. In these schools, such as Huntington Woods Elementary in Wyoming, Michigan, LABBB Collaborative School in Lexington, Massachusetts, and Lake Gibson Middle School in Lakeland, Florida, no one bosses anyone and lead-management flourishes. In these schools, students are being trained in the ideas of choice theory because the staff have discovered that the more students know about how they function, the better they tend to behave.

I also have feedback from the many teachers in other schools who have become skilled in the use of reality therapy and choice theory and have taught these skills to students. They have discovered that students have no difficulty learning these ideas. They catch on quickly to the fact that they have needs they must satisfy and that they choose the behaviors they use to satisfy them. Once they do, they stop blaming others for their problems and start working on making better choices in their own lives. Students become especially intrigued with the idea that they have quality worlds inside their heads and see the value of working with their teachers to keep schoolwork in these worlds. In a quality school a systematic effort would be made, starting in the first grade with the concept of the needs, to teach all students choice theory and how to use it in their lives.

While every concept in this book is based on the ideas of choice theory and reality therapy, neither a book nor a training course can tell a school exactly how to implement these ideas. For example, when and how should a school break with the traditional system of grades and move to the system suggested in Chapter Eight? This is something that each school has to work out for itself. Teachers would have to decide when this was a good move to make and how to make it. Students and parents would have to be involved and a school board persuaded that it was in the best interests of the students.

During the first year, when many small changes would start to take place, I do not think it would be a good idea to involve the students in much discussion about what was happening. Like teachers, students are quite skeptical when "great changes" are announced, and this skepticism would hamper the process. For example, the two most important practices of a quality school are ending coercion and beginning student self-evaluation. As I will discuss next, both should be started as soon as the decision is made to begin, but neither need be announced as being part of a "big deal" process that is now getting started. If these practices work well, and students and teachers support them, they will speak adequately for themselves. Then, because they have been accepted, they can be mentioned and their vital role in a quality school explained.

STUDENT SELF-EVALUATION

While most teachers and administrators will require training if they are to manage students without coercion, little or no special training is needed to persuade students that it is to their benefit to evaluate their work. As covered extensively in Chapter Seven, we all know quality when we see it, but students in a quality school need to be alerted to look for it much more than they do now. Teachers should begin by talking to students in a general way about the subject of quality. They might use a course that all students take, like social studies or history, so that all are exposed to a similar discussion. Each teacher must figure out for herself the best way to do this, but I suggest spending part of several periods on the subject. After this introduction, all teachers involved in the process should spend a few minutes each day talking about quality so that students get the idea that evaluating the quality of what they do, both in and out of school, is now a high-priority goal.

Ask students to look for quality in how they dress, how they wear their hair, the language they choose to express themselves, the music and the movies they like, what they watch on television, what is advertised, and what they buy. After they develop an appreciation of quality in these areas of their lives, move into a discussion of what it takes to be seen as a quality person. Ask them to use history and current events for examples of quality people, and try to get them to see that they judge some people as having much more quality than others. Ask them to tell you why they made these judgments, and then discuss with them what may be some of the criteria for human quality. As you talk to each other informally at lunch and at breaks, share what you have learned in these quality discussions and help each other to become more skillful in this new area of teaching and awareness.

Once students are acutely aware of what quality is, ask them to think about quality as it applies to school. Is there quality in the subjects they take and in the assignments they are asked to do? If they do not see quality in the subjects they take, or if they see it in the subjects but not in the assignments that are given in these subjects, ask how more quality could be injected into what they do in school. Try to explain how to find quality, for example, in math, science, English, and history. This is not an easy task; you will have to do it in small segments as you continue teaching, but there is no hurry. Go slowly and students will remain interested. It takes time for this new idea to gel. You are aiming to have students see the quality of what you ask them to do. If they cannot see this, they will never do the high-level work that is the core of a quality school.

As you do this, ask students to take the next necessary step, which is to begin to judge some of what they do in school for quality. Use classroom assignments rather than homework, as many students do not do their homework. See if they would be willing to evaluate in writing the quality of one of their assignments. Discuss what to write on the top of the paper to indicate the evaluation. For example, it could be a grade, a number, or the words "high quality," "average quality" or "low quality." After you have agreed on a designation, ask students to try evaluating their work.

Make sure the first time you do this that what you assign is clear-cut enough so that judging the quality is easy. For example, assign them to write a paragraph describing their favorite television show and then judge what they wrote for quality before turning it in. Tell students that you are very serious about this process and that you are going to begin to keep two records of the quality of what they do: your evaluation and theirs. Tell them that you will do this as soon as you are convinced that they are making a serious effort to judge the quality of all they do. This means that their grades on future assignments (not tests) will be based on both your judgment and their judgment of their work.

During the second part of the first year of the quality school program, have students begin to evaluate every aspect of the school in which they are involved. For example, regardless of how anyone else evaluates what they do, what is their evaluation of their participation in extracurricular activities? How do they judge their effort to keep the school clean, help other students, help teachers, spread the idea that their school is a good place to learn, and any other aspect of school that you or they can think of?

You are trying to get students to judge the quality of the life they are choosing to lead. They are used to judging the quality of others and having others judge them. It is judging themselves that will be new, and this judgment is vital. Unless students begin to do this on a regular basis, it will be very difficult to move to a quality school.

Try to teach students this important lesson: The success or the failure of our lives is greatly dependent on our willingness to judge the quality of what we do and then to improve it if we find it wanting. But during the first year do not focus on what students could do to improve their lives. Until coercion can be eliminated from the school, they may see your asking them to improve as coercive. If they ask whether you are interested in their improving the quality of what they do, tell them that your main interest is that they judge their performance; improving it is up to them. Actually, you may never have to focus on improvement because, driven by our need for power, once we become aware of a shortcoming, we cannot help trying to improve. If all the teachers who have made the commitment to a quality school do what is suggested here for at least a semester, they will be well on their way to a quality school.

This should not be difficult to do. You are not asking students to do anything that takes a great deal of time or effort. Once they get used to doing this, it is amazingly easy to make these judgments. It may not be easy for your students to live with their evaluations if they are low, but that is not your problem. It is their problem, which is the purpose of doing this. As a lead-manager, however, you will offer help if students want to improve, which most of them will want to do. The more they want to improve, the less you will feel that you must push them. The urge to coerce will thus be greatly reduced by this self-evaluation plan. There will also be less work for you when your students get involved in these evaluations and do better work. It should also be fun. There is grist for many good discussions and laughs as you struggle with students in this new direction.

INVOLVING ALL THE STUDENTS IN QUALITY LEARNING

In any school there are students who not only do not do quality work, but in fact do no work at all. We now try to rectify this problem by setting up special programs to "fix" these low performers, many of whom are diagnosed as having a mental or emotional handicap, although research fails to confirm this diagnosis.[3] By introducing more need-satisfying classes, we should be able to persuade most of these students to start doing much more in school and to gain the confidence to attempt to do quality work. Keep in mind that these will be the students who will be most resistant to evaluating their work, who will be immune to coercive discipline, and for whom quality schoolwork is a foreign idea.

Identifying these students should be easy; it is well known who is working and who is not. Once they have been identified, they must be persuaded to start working much harder than most do now. To do this, a teacher, counselor, or administrator should follow up the quality discussions the students are exposed to in class with a personal interview or even a series of short personal interviews about quality. Using no threat, ask each student the following question: "We believe you can do more than you are doing: What do you think about doing something of quality in school?"

Many will try to convince you that they are satisfied with the way things are now. They say this because they do not believe that they could do much better in this school, and they do not want to expend energy in what, to them, is a lost cause. For many, the whole idea of doing quality work is overwhelming. They have no recent experience of doing well in school, and the question does not make much sense to them.

The key here is to begin to focus quickly; quality schoolwork is too abstract a concept for these students to follow. Ask, "Is there any part of any of your classes that you consider valuable enough to work hard and do quality work?" Gently and with encouragement, the teacher, counselor, administrator, peer counselor, or volunteer must keep asking this question over and over in a variety of ways until the student agrees to do a very small amount of what he or she considers quality work. Here the teacher has to figure out how to exhibit persistent interest that the student will see as caring rather than nagging or pressuring. To be more persuasive, the teacher should offer to help the student to get started or arrange to get a tutor involved.

Someone must persist in this even if it means going to the students' homes and talking about it in front of their parents or whoever is there. For these students the point must be made that we care and are going to show that caring actively and in ways that we have not shown it before. For home visits, I suggest that the school put together "quality teams" made up of students who are doing some quality work, along with a staff member or volunteer. The teams might wear T-shirts inscribed with the words, "I am a member of the Hudson High Quality Team."

When they find that people from the school will not give up, that quality teams come right to their homes or wherever they can find them, students will be impressed. They cannot help thinking that the school cares and has confidence in them, that they are being given a choice they have never been offered before, and that the question is not coercive. To help them to see the value of working, it may be a good idea to talk to them about whether they want to graduate. Argue gently that graduation is worthwhile and that they can go further in life if they get involved in the quality that the school is now talking about.

If you are persistent, students will eventually say that they are interested in doing something that they judge has quality. Then a plan has to be made with the teacher of the subject in which they want to do quality work. Anything of quality should be acceptable, no matter how little, because what is needed to get nonworkers started is for them to do one piece of quality work. It is a beginning. After they have done one assignment well, they will feel some of the power that goes with quality, and it will be easier to help them plan to do more and start evaluating all of their work.

If these students start to succeed, ask them to join a quality team that visits other students. When the low-achievers, who tend to know each other, see a former low-achiever on a quality team, it will be very persuasive.

BEGINNING TO ELIMINATE COERCION AND CRITICISM

Even before anyone takes the formal training in choice theory and reality therapy that will focus on dealing with students and teachers without coercion, the staff should start eliminating coercion from all they do. For dealing with students, use the examples in Chapters Nine and Ten. When students break a rule or fail to exert effort, tell them that you will work with them to help them figure out how to solve what is obviously a problem. Where rules are concerned, emphasize that you will no longer threaten or punish, but you will not be able to keep a student in class who is not willing to work with you to follow the rules.

Ask your students to help you by pointing out when they think you are threatening or when you criticize them personally. When they point out a slip, ask what you could have said or done instead. Not only will they be amazingly sensitive in this area, but they will also be creative in suggesting alternatives. Most students know what teachers should say instead of the coercive remarks we tend to use, but they never tell us because we usually never ask.

Tell students that you want to be their friend, not their adversary, and then make a point of showing this in all you do. Let them know that you want to help them do what both you and they agree is quality work, but you need their help. You cannot teach the way they would like if they are not willing to get actively involved in the process.

COOPERATIVE LEARNING

When the superintendent approached me for help, he told me that cooperative learning was already a significant component of the school program because he was well aware that this is a very need-satisfying way to teach and learn. This method has been covered extensively in *Choice Theory in the Classroom* and need not be repeated here, except to say that it is hard to visualize any quality school that is not deeply involved in this method of instruction. A quality school would make training in this method available to all interested teachers. In fact, I recognize now what I failed to see when I wrote *Choice Theory in the Classroom*, which is that cooperative learning has been slow to catch on because it is so difficult for boss-managers to give students the control over their work that is inherent in this method of instruction. In a lead-managed quality school, cooperative learning should flourish.

GOVERNING THE QUALITY SCHOOL

Lead-management should extend to student and parent participation in the government of a quality school. While there should be elections for half the students who serve on the student-faculty-parent association that should govern the school, the other half should be selected differently. All students who want to serve on this body, or on a separate student council that gives recommendations to this body, should put their names in a hat, and the ones drawn should be selected. This would give the less popular students a chance to have a say in the running of the school that they would never get if they had to be elected. The meetings of the governing body should be open to all who are interested, and anyone should have a chance to speak. At least once a semester a town meeting, open to all, should be held to discuss school concerns. All major changes in the way the school was governed should be voted upon at this meeting.

NAME TAGS

An effort should be made to increase the number of people in the school who know each other by name. People who call each other by name work together much better and become friends much faster. To accomplish this, the faculty might agree that they, and all adults in the school on school business, will wear name tags. This would set an example and encourage students to do the same. The name tags could be creative, standard, or both. To encourage students to wear them, prizes could be given for the most creative tags. A student without a name tag would be asked to put one on, and teachers should have a supply of temporary tags to hand out to students who need them.

While it should not be compulsory to wear a name tag, every effort should be made to persuade all to do so. No teacher would then have to talk to a student without knowing his or her name. This simple procedure, more than anything else that can be done, would reduce discipline problems. The students should be encouraged to wear their name tags in the community, and some businesses might be persuaded to give discounts to students wearing their name tags.

BONUSES FOR SUCCESS

When the quality of the work increases, as it will in a lead-managed school, it will be because the workers and the managers are working together much better than before. They should be compensated for this effort. The fairest way to do this is to award a financial bonus to the whole school for any obvious increase in quality, but this bonus should be totally excluded from all salary negotiations. While I cannot give an exact formula for this bonus, it seems fair to compare past and present records and relate the award to how close the school comes to reaching the following quality school goals:

1. Students do not leave school; the dropout rate is essentially zero.
2. Student attendance is almost perfect; tardiness and absence disappear.
3. Teacher absenteeism goes significantly below the average for the state.
4. There are no discipline problems that are not quickly and easily solved.
5. The records show that all students have achieved competence or beyond in what are considered hard courses, like math and science, and substantial numbers of students took courses at what would be considered college level. These numbers should be far more than what is achieved in comparable, boss-managed schools.
6. There are few or no diagnoses of learning disabilities.
7. There is significantly less student delinquency in the community the school serves as reported by the police and juvenile agencies.

To the extent that there are significant improvements since the school began the move to quality and a bonus is awarded, I suggest that 75 percent of the money be divided equally among the faculty and 25 percent be used for the direct benefit of students. Even the faculty who did not actively participate in the program should share in the bonus as it is unlikely that any faculty member would remain completely uninvolved if the school began to reach these goals.

As the goals are reached, the community the school serves would save a substantial amount of money, and a representative of the teachers should work with the community financial officer to accurately assess the actual amount of this saving. The bonus should be paid out of this sum. If all the goals listed above were reached, both the sum and the bonus to the teachers should be substantial. The student bonus should be used to improve the school plant and equipment, send students on trips, award scholarships, and pay students who tutor other students a small fee. These are only suggestions; the student-faculty-parent governing body would make the actual decisions.

SUMMARY

None of the ideas in this book is beyond the capability of any school in the country right now if the leadership is willing to do the work to make the move. Just as there is nothing wrong with American workers, there is nothing wrong with our students. Deming was right; it is the way we manage them that must be changed. By the end of the first year, if most of the coercion has been removed from the school and most of the students are evaluating what they do in school, the move to quality will be well underway. Much hard work will remain, however, as the staff gets involved in the training. The ideas in this book are only the basics. Much more will be added and refined by each school as the staff is trained and the payoff for the move to quality becomes more and more apparent.

Nothing we can do will improve the quality of life in any community more than quality schools. Young people who are involved in quality education do not engage in self-destructive activities and are an asset to the community. And since most industries can now be located almost anywhere, good schools are a major incentive for an industry to move to a community. There is no more effective and economical way to improve the economy of a community than for it to become known for excellent schools.

I look forward to an increasing number of quality schools and ultimately a Quality School Association that maintains the standards, helps other schools to make the move to quality, and sends out committees to evaluate schools that believe they are ready for the official designation, Quality School. My vision is a quality flag flying below the American flag on the flagpoles of an increasing number of schools. I invite you to share that vision.

Notes

PREFACE

1. Shayle does not know the source of this material. If any reader knows, we will be happy to attribute it properly in a future printing.

CHAPTER ONE. Quality Education Is the Only
Answer to Our School Problems

1. Further information about Deming is published in Dr. Myron Tribus, *Selected Papers on Quality and Productivity Improvement*. This book can be obtained by sending $15 to the National Society of Professional Engineers, P.O. Box 96163, Washington, D.C. 20090–6163.

2. See the article by James Risen, *Los Angeles Times*, May 20, 1989, pp. 1, 18.

3. *Los Angeles Times*, February 1, 1989, p. 4.

4. W. Edwards Deming, *Out of the Crisis* (Cambridge: Massachusetts Institute of Technology, Center for Advanced Engineering Study, 1982).

5. National Commission on Excellence in Education, *A Nation at Risk: The Imperative for Educational Reform* (Washington, D.C.: U.S. Government Printing Office, 1983).

6. Linda M. McNeil, *Contradictions of Control: School Structure and School Knowledge* (New York: Routledge, 1986).

7. *Los Angeles Times*, April 27, 1989, Metro Section, p. 1.

8. William Glasser, *Choice Theory in the Classroom* (New York: HarperCollins 1998), formerly called *Control Theory in the Classroom.*

CHAPTER TWO. Effective Teaching May Be the Hardest Job There Is

1. See Chapter One, note 6.
2. Linda M. McNeil, *Phi Delta Kappan*, March 1988, p. 485.
3. Linda M. McNeil, *Phi Delta Kappan*, January 1988, p. 337.

CHAPTER THREE. We Need Noncoercive Lead-management from the State Superintendent to the Teacher

1. A good review of the research on what is essentially lead-management (he calls it "system 4") is included in Rensis Likert, *Past and Future Perspectives on System 4*, 1977. This paper can be obtained from Rensis Likert Association Inc., 630 City Center Building, Ann Arbor, MI 48104.

2. Ellen Flax, "New Dropout Data Highlights Problems in the Middle Years," *Education Week*, Vol. VIII, No. 30, April 19, 1989.

3. See Chapter One, note 4.

CHAPTER FOUR. Choice Theory and Motivation

1. Stanley M. Elam, "The Second Gallup/Phi Delta Kappa Poll," *Phi Delta Kappan*, June 1989, p. 787.

2. Ron Harris, *Los Angeles Times*, May 29, 1989, p. 1.

CHAPTER SIX. How We Behave: Quality Work Feels Good

1. See the major book on choice theory: *Choice Theory: A New Psychology of Personal Freedom* (New York: HarperCollins, 1998).

CHAPTER SEVEN. Quality Schoolwork

1. See McNeil, *Contradictions of Control,* for documentation of this claim.

2. Robert Pirsig, *Zen and the Art of Motorcycle Maintenance* (New York: Morrow, 1974).

CHAPTER EIGHT. Grades and Other Basics of a Quality School

1. Jay Matthews, *Escalante: The Best Teacher in America* (New York: Henry Holt, 1988), p. 271.

2. This is a test given by the Educational Testing Service (ETS) in Princeton, New Jersey. A score of 3 or better (5 is the top score) qualifies a student to take a higher level course in that subject in college.

3. See Chapter Four, note 1.

CHAPTER NINE. Building a Friendly Workplace

1. One of the best volunteer programs was initiated by Bill Borgers, former superintendent of the Dickinson, Texas, School District, and now on staff at Houston Baptist College in Houston, Texas. Contact Bill in Houston if you want some hints on how to get a volunteer program started.

CHAPTER TEN. Dealing with Discipline Problems

1. See Chapter Nine, note 1.

CHAPTER ELEVEN. Creating the Quality School

1. Mary Walton, *The Deming Management Method* (New York: Perigee Books, 1986), p. 35.

2. Training in reality therapy and choice theory is available through the William Glasser Institute 22024 Lassen Street, Suite 118, Chatsworth, CA 91311.

3. Gerald Coles, *The Learning Mystique* (New York: Pantheon, 1988).